MACROS
made easy

60 Quick and Delicious Recipes
for Hitting Your Protein, Fat and Carb Goals

DANIELLE LIMA, Creator of Oh Snap Macros

PAGE STREET
PUBLISHING CO.

PAGE STREET
PUBLISHING CO.

First published in 2024 by

Page Street Publishing Co.

27 Congress Street, Suite 1511

Salem, MA 01970

www.pagestreetpublishing.com

Distributed by Macmillan, sales in Canada by The Canadian Manda Group.

28   27   26   25   24   1   2   3   4   5

ISBN-13: 978-1-64567-863-2

ISBN-10: 1-64567-863-6

Library of Congress Control Number: 2023936639

Cover and book design by Meg Baskis for Page Street Publishing Co.

Food photography by Danielle Lima, lifestyle photography by Jami Aafedt

Printed and bound in the United States of America

dedication

For my precious girls, Katherine and Madison, who fill my life with joy and purpose, and my beloved Mom, whose love and guidance continues to inspire me—this cookbook is for you.

contents

INTRODUCTION

Hi, I'm Danielle! First and foremost, I want to thank you for purchasing this cookbook! I am beyond grateful that you are putting your trust in me and my recipes to provide you with delicious, easy meals that bring a table full of smiles along with them. I never thought I would have the opportunity to write a cookbook, nor did I think the small blog I started so long ago would grow into such a warm and welcoming community. I truly appreciate each and every one of you who has made Oh Snap Macros what it is today.

A little about me: I am a wife, mom to two little girls and creator of OhSnapMacros.com, a macro-friendly food blog. After gaining more than 80 pounds while pregnant with my second daughter, I discovered a love for macros: focusing on them has helped me nourish my body in ways that are best suited for me. I lost some of the baby weight by tracking my macros, and I added strength training and learned I love eating high-protein meals and lifting heavy weights.

In 2022, I quit my full-time corporate job to pursue my dream of cooking and creating—and that is how Oh Snap Macros evolved. My mission is to have my recipes be easy and also to have them surprise you. I want you to finish a meal and think, *wow, that was macro friendly?* Bonus points if your family and friends love it too. Triple points if I can make tracking macros easy and fun. These recipes are not only for people tracking macros; they're also designed to be delicious for everyone and, ultimately, family friendly.

So, what are macros? Macros boil down to your three key macronutrients: protein, carbohydrates and fat. Tracking your macros is balancing these three macronutrients according to your goals. Those goals look different for each person, and they can range from fat loss to maintaining current weight or even eating in a surplus to build muscle. People with health concerns might also track their macros and focus on limiting or increasing a specific macronutrient.

There are endless ways to get these three macronutrients into each meal in a balanced way—and that's where this book comes into play. I am going to help you hit your macro goals with delicious and easy recipes using everyday, common ingredients to make tracking macros easy for you.

As you make the recipes, please keep in mind that the nutrition facts are estimated based on the ingredients used in the recipe; they may vary slightly depending on the specific brands and measurements you use. Use the nutrition facts I have included as a guide, and note that it's always a good idea to calculate the nutrition for your specific ingredients to get the most accurate information. See the following sections for further information on this. Happy cooking!

Cheers,

Danielle Sinna

Tracking Macros Tips and Tricks

As a food blogger and fitness enthusiast, I often get asked about the best way to track macros. Macros, short for macronutrients, are the building blocks of our diets and include carbohydrates, proteins and fats. Each macro plays a unique role in our body, and understanding how to balance them can be the key to achieving optimal health and fitness. In this chapter, I explain what macros are and the benefits of tracking them.

What Are Macros?

Macros are the three main nutrients that our bodies need to function properly. They are:

- **Carbohydrates**—Carbs are our primary source of energy. They are found in foods such as fruits, vegetables, grains and sugars.

- **Proteins**—Proteins are essential for building and repairing tissues in our bodies. They are found in foods such as meats, fish, eggs and beans.

- **Fats**—Fats are important for hormone regulation, insulation and energy storage. They are found in foods such as nuts, seeds, oils and butter.

Each macro plays a critical role in our bodies, and the key to optimal health is to balance them in the right proportions. Nutrition labels include macros: simply search for the protein, carbs and fats on the label.

The ideal macronutrient ratios can vary from person to person, depending on factors such as age, weight, activity level, health goals, health concerns and food preferences. To calculate your ideal macronutrient ratios, start by determining your maintenance calories or your total daily energy expenditure (TDEE). To get an accurate estimate, you can use a TDEE online calculator or consult with a certified nutritionist. You also can use the official Oh Snap Macros app (see page 154) to help you create meal plans and to customize your week to meet all your macro needs!

The Benefits of Tracking Your Macros

Once you know your maintenance calorie needs, you can calculate your ideal macro ratios based on your goals, whether it be to maintain, lose fat or bulk. Tracking your macros can have many benefits, including:

- **Better weight management:** Tracking macros can help you achieve your weight goals, whether it's weight loss, maintenance or to gain muscle. By understanding your daily caloric intake and adjusting your macros accordingly, you can create a tailored nutrition plan to meet your specific needs.

- **Improved body composition:** Tracking macros can help you achieve a better balance of muscle and fat in your body. By consuming the right amount of protein, you can support muscle growth while losing fat.

- **Enhanced athletic performance:** Athletes need the right balance of macros to fuel their bodies for optimal performance. Tracking macros can help ensure that you're consuming an appropriate balance of nutrients to support your training and recovery.

- **Greater dietary awareness:** Tracking your macros can make you more conscious of what you're eating, helping you make healthier food choices and develop better eating habits.
- **Better management of dietary needs:** For those with specific dietary needs, such as managing diabetes or other health conditions, tracking macros can help maintain a balanced diet that meets your nutritional requirements.
- **Easier meal planning:** Knowing your macro goals can simplify meal planning, allowing you to create meals that fit your nutritional needs and preferences.
- **Increased energy levels:** Consuming the right balance of macros can help maintain consistent energy levels throughout the day, preventing energy crashes and improving overall well-being.
- **Adaptability:** Tracking macros allows you to adjust your diet based on changing circumstances, such as increased physical activity or new health goals.

By tracking your macronutrients, you can gain valuable insight into your eating habits and make informed decisions to optimize your diet for better health and performance.

How to Track Your Macros

Once you have calculated your ideal macronutrient ratios, the next step is to track your macros. This can be done using food-tracking apps or even a simple pen and paper, but I definitely suggest using an app for ease. They offer a streamlined and efficient approach to achieving nutrition goals. These apps serve as powerful tools that reduce the hassle of manual calculations, making it easier for users to understand and adjust their intake of proteins, fats and carbohydrates. My favorite apps to use are MyFitnessPal™ and Macros-First. You can find all of these and more recipes logged into both apps for easy tracking. Just search in their "all recipes" section for "MME," followed by the recipe name to log the recipes in this book with your daily macros. If you want help meal planning using these recipes, be sure to check out my app, Oh Snap Macros, in the app store.

To track your macros effectively: Start by weighing and measuring your food portions using a food scale. This will help you get an accurate estimate of the macronutrients in your meals.

When tracking your macros, it's also essential to read food labels and know the macronutrient content of the foods you eat. This will help you make informed choices and ensure you are staying within your ideal macro ratios. Make sure you're reading the labels, taking note of the serving size and weighing all your ingredients! This will help you get the most accurate measurements for your food and macros.

Why Weigh Your Ingredients and Portions?

Eyeballing your measurements can vastly vary your calories. For example, imagine if you log 1 cup (163 g) of cooked basmati rice in your tracking app, but you used the uncooked nutrition facts instead? One cup (178 g) of uncooked basmati rice is 640 calories versus 1 cup of cooked basmati rice is 220 calories—which can make a huge difference in the accuracy of your macros and calories.

Imagine if you didn't weigh out your uncooked basmati and instead packed it inside 1 cup and ended up with double the serving? It's important to read the labels to confirm the weight per serving so you're accurate. For example, raw meat and potatoes on average lose 25 percent of their weight when cooked—without losing any macronutrients, just weight.

To help you easily convert ingredients from raw to cooked and vice versa, here are a few useful calculation estimates.

Meat and Potatoes

- Raw to Cooked = Raw Weight × 0.75
- Cooked to Raw = Cooked Weight ÷ 0.75

Pasta will increase on average by 2.25 times its weight once it is cooked.

- Raw to Cooked = Raw Weight × 2.25
- Cooked to Raw = Cooked Weight ÷ 2.25

Brown Rice will increase on average by 2 times its weight once it is cooked.

- Raw to Cooked = Raw Weight × 2
- Cooked to Raw = Cooked Weight ÷ 2

White Rice will increase on average by 3 times its weight once it is cooked.

- Raw to Cooked = Raw Weight × 3
- Cooked to Raw = Cooked Weight ÷ 3

Weighing Servings

For the most accurate serving size, I always recommend people weigh out their total cooked food and divide by the serving size listed. There are a few ways to do that:

To calculate servings of cooked food: Set a large plate or bowl on a scale and zero it out. Add the cooked food to the dish for the total weight of the cooked food. Divide that number by the number of servings and that is your total weight per serving.

- Total weight of food = 1,000 grams (excluding the dish)
- Total servings = 10 servings
- 1,000 ÷ 10 = 100 grams per serving

To calculate servings prior to cooking: This is especially great for bakes, pastas and soups. Weigh your empty dish prior to filling it and cooking the meal. Turn on your scale and weigh the dish you will use to cook the meal. Write it down on a piece of paper or on your phone notes to save for later.

Once your meal is cooked, turn on the scale, and add the cooked meal in the same dish you weighed earlier to the scale for the total overall cooked weight. Subtract the empty dish weight from the total cooked weight for your total grams of food. Divide this number by the total servings listed.

- Empty dish: 1,500 grams
- Cooked meal in the same dish: 3,500 grams
- 3,500 - 1,500 = 2,000 grams (of food only)
- Total Servings: 8 servings
- 2,000 ÷ 8 = 250 grams per serving

Recipe Glossary: Making Your Macros Work for You

Let this recipe glossary be your guide to navigating recipes that are high protein, low carb, low fat and macro balanced. These collections have been designed to help you navigate the world of fitting recipes into your personal macros with ease. Need something that's high in protein? Scan this list and get cooking!

High-Protein Recipes: More Than 35 Grams per Serving

Sun-Dried Tomato and Arugula Burgers

Grill to Table

Calories: 478 | Protein: 52 | Carbs: 37 | Total Fat: 15

Creamy Blackberry Steak Salad

Bowls and Handhelds

Calories: 368 | Protein: 43 | Carbs: 17 | Total Fat: 14

Grilled Blackened Chicken Caesar Cobb Salad

Bowls and Handhelds

Calories: 330 | Protein: 42 | Carbs: 9 | Total Fat: 14

Dad's Jambalaya

One-Pan Weeknight Winners

Calories: 382 | Protein: 41 | Carbs: 31 | Total Fat: 10

One-Pan Chicken Fajita Pasta

Easy Pasta in Just 30 Minutes

Calories: 362 | Protein: 39 | Carbs: 32 | Total Fat: 9

Jerk Chicken Bowls

Bowls and Handhelds

Calories: 359 | Protein: 39 | Carbs: 39 | Total Fat: 5

Shrimp Fried Rice

One-Pan Weeknight Winners

Calories: 365 | Protein: 39 | Carbs: 36 | Total Fat: 7

Peanut Chicken Skewers

Grill to Table

Calories: 263 | Protein: 38 | Carbs: 28 | Total Fat: 9

Peanut Chicken Stir-Fry

One-Pan Weeknight Winners

Calories: 348 | Protein: 38 | Carbs: 28 | Total Fat: 9

Chipotle Chicken Pasta

Easy Pasta in Just 30 Minutes

Calories: 404 | Protein: 37 | Carbs: 51 | Total Fat: 6

Chicken Caesar Burger

Grill to Table

Calories: 395 | Protein: 36 | Carbs: 34 | Total Fat: 19

Cheesy Sausage Frittata

Best Ever Breakfasts

Calories: 112 | Protein: 15 | Carbs: 1 | Total Fat: 5

Cajun Shrimp and Sausage Kabobs

Grill to Table

Calories: 130 | Protein: 23 | Carbs: 1 | Total Fat: 6

Blackened Chicken Breast

Grill to Table

Calories: 137 | Protein: 23 | Carbs: 2 | Total Fat: 4

Creamy Mediterranean Halibut

One-Pan Weeknight Winners

Calories: 187 | Protein: 25 | Carbs: 5 | Total Fat: 8

Marinated Steak with Sweet-and-Spicy Chimichurri

Grill to Table

Calories: 235 | Protein: 24 | Carbs: 6 | Total Fat: 13

Cast-Iron Taco Pie

One-Pan Weeknight Winners

Calories: 147 | Protein: 18 | Carbs: 6 | Total Fat: 5

Sunday Quiche

Best Ever Breakfasts

Calories: 240 | Protein: 19 | Carbs: 7 | Total Fat: 14

Buffalo Chicken Stuffed Peppers

Bowls and Handhelds

Calories: 167 | Protein: 21 | Carbs: 8 | Total Fat: 5

Loaded Cauli Mash

Showstopping Sides

Calories: 140 | Protein: 15 | Carbs: 8 | Total Fat: 6

Grilled Blackened Chicken Caesar Cobb Salad

Bowls and Handhelds

Calories: 330 | Protein: 42 | Carbs: 9 | Total Fat: 14

Honey-Garlic Shrimp Skewers

Grill to Table

Calories: 136 | Protein: 17 | Carbs: 9 | Total Fat: 14

Classic Coleslaw

Showstopping Sides

Calories: 70 | Protein: 5 | Carbs: 9 | Total Fat: 2

Hawaiian Pineapple Shrimp Scampi

Easy Pasta in Just 30 Minutes

Calories: 163 | Protein: 21 | Carbs: 10 | Total Fat: 3

Fancy Green Beans

Showstopping Sides

Calories: 99 | Protein: 3 | Carbs: 10 | Total Fat: 6

Banana Cream Puff Pancakes

Best Ever Breakfasts

Calories: 98 | Protein: 9 | Carbs: 13 | Total Fat: 2

Spicy Shrimp Tacos and Mango Slaw

Bowls and Handhelds

Calories: 127 | Protein: 11 | Carbs: 16 | Total Fat: 2

Hidden Veggie One-Pot Spaghetti

Easy Pasta in Just 30 Minutes

Calories: 314 | Protein: 31 | Carbs: 45 | Total Fat: 2

Hawaiian Pineapple Shrimp Scampi

Easy Pasta in Just 30 Minutes

Calories: 163 | Protein: 21 | Carbs: 10 | Total Fat: 3

Roasted Garlic Cottage Mashed Potatoes

Showstopping Sides

Calories: 140 | Protein: 4 | Carbs: 26 | Total Fat: 3

Mom's "Best Ever" Peanut Noodles

Showstopping Sides

Calories: 205 | Protein: 9 | Carbs: 36 | Total Fat: 3

Harvest Breakfast Bowls with Creamy Dijon Sauce

Best Ever Breakfasts

Calories: 273 | Protein: 11 | Carbs: 47 | Total Fat: 4

High-Protein Baked Beans

Showstopping Sides

Calories: 197 | Protein: 14 | Carbs: 28 | Total Fat: 4

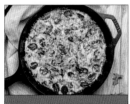

Cheesy Sausage Frittata

Best Ever Breakfasts

Calories: 112 | Protein: 15 | Carbs: 1 | Total Fat: 5

Buffalo Chicken Stuffed Peppers

Bowls and Handhelds

Calories: 167 | Protein: 21 | Carbs: 8 | Total Fat: 5

Peanut Chicken Skewers

Grill to Table

Calories: 263 | Protein: 38 | Carbs: 12 | Total Fat: 5

Blackened Chicken Salad

Bowls and Handhelds

Calories: 222 | Protein: 30 | Carbs: 14 | Total Fat: 5

Blackened Salmon Fajitas

One-Pan Weeknight Winners

Calories: 118 | Protein: 10 | Carbs: 17 | Total Fat: 5

Spicy Chicken Tacos with Creamy Apple Slaw

Bowls and Handhelds

Calories: 152 | Protein: 11 | Carbs: 19 | Total Fat: 3

Cinnamon Apple French Toast Casserole

Best Ever Breakfasts

Calories: 306 | Protein: 23 | Carbs: 42 | Total Fat: 5

Peanut Chicken Skewers

Grill to Table

Calories: 263 | Protein: 38 |
Carbs: 12 | Total Fat: 5

Low-Carb Beef "Noodles"

Easy Pasta in Just 30 Minutes

Calories: 337 | Protein: 33 |
Carbs: 26 | Total Fat: 11

**Creamy Green Chicken
Enchilada Soup**

One-Pan Weeknight Winners

Calories: 285 | Protein: 33 |
Carbs: 21 | Total Fat: 7

Blackened Chicken Salad

Bowls and Handhelds

Calories: 222 | Protein: 30 |
Carbs: 14 | Total Fat: 5

**Macro-Friendly Instant Pot
Chili**

One-Pan Weeknight Winners

Calories: 241 | Protein: 28 |
Carbs: 22 | Total Fat: 6

Beef and Broccoli

Bowls and Handhelds

Calories: 213 | Protein: 28 |
Carbs: 12 | Total Fat: 6

Mom's Chunky Beef Stew

One-Pan Weeknight Winners

Calories: 252 | Protein: 27 |
Carbs: 16 | Total Fat: 7

Blackened Chicken Breast

Grill to Table

Calories: 137 | Protein: 26 |
Carbs: 2 | Total Fat: 4

**Creamy Mediterranean
Halibut**

One-Pan Weeknight Winners

Calories: 187 | Protein: 25 |
Carbs: 5 | Total Fat: 8

**Cinnamon Apple French
Toast Casserole**

Best Ever Breakfasts

Calories: 306 | Protein: 23 |
Carbs: 42 | Total Fat: 5

**Chipotle Breakfast
Sandwich**

Best Ever Breakfasts

Calories: 241 | Protein: 20 |
Carbs: 26 | Total Fat: 9

Sides and Volume Adds

Not sure what to pair with Blackened Chicken Breast (page 122) or Cajun Shrimp and Sausage Kabobs (page 113)? Here you'll find a list of sides to help you put together your meals. Whether you're looking for something that's high carb, low carb or just containing a specific calorie count, this list will help you get there.

What is a volume add? Volume foods are typically added to meals to increase their overall volume without adding many calories or unwanted macronutrients. These volume foods are typically low in calories but high in fiber, meaning they can make you feel full without contributing a significant amount of energy to your diet. Examples of such foods include vegetables such as lettuce, zucchini, spaghetti squash and broccoli.

Please note that all nutrition facts in this section have been pulled from MyFitnessPal™ and/or specific brand and product websites at the time of writing.

- White medium-grain rice (1 cup cooked [187 g]) = 5 g protein | 53 g carbs | 0 g fat | 242 calories
- Basmati rice (1 cup cooked [180 g]) = 5 g protein | 46 g carbs | 0 g fat | 205 calories
- Brown rice (1 cup cooked [195 g]) = 5 g protein | 46 g carbs | 2 g fat | 218 calories
- Jasmine rice (1 cup cooked [158 g]) = 4 g protein | 45 g carbs | 0 g fat | 205 calories

Instead of rice try:

- Cauliflower rice (1 cup cooked [100 g]) = 2 g protein | 5 g carbs | 0 g fat | 25 calories
- Combination basmati rice and cauli (1 cup each [280 g]) = 7 g protein | 51 g carbs | 1 g fat | 230 calories
- Farro (1 cup cooked [100 g]) = 11 g protein | 50 g carbs | 0 g fat | 242 calories
- Chickpea rice (¼ cup dry [50 g]) = 15 g protein | 40 g carbs | 4 g fat | 269 calories
- Quinoa (1 cup cooked [185 g]) = 8 g protein | 40 g carbs | 4 g fat | 222 calories
- Cabbage (1 cup shredded [70 g]) = 1 g protein | 4 g carbs | 0 g fat | 18 calories
- Broccoli (1 cup chopped [128 g]) = 3 g protein | 6 g carbs | 0 g fat | 30 calories
- Spaghetti (2 oz dry [57 g]) = 7 g protein | 42 g carbs | 1 g fat | 200 calories

Instead of pasta try:

- Banza™ pasta (2 oz dry [57 g]) = 11 g protein | 35 g carbs | 3 g fat | 190 calories
- Barilla® spaghetti (Protein Plus; 2 oz dry [57 g]) = 10 g protein | 39 g carbs | 1 g fat | 190 calories
- Zoodles (1 cup [85 g]) = 1 protein | 8 g carbs | 3 g fat | 15 calories
- Shirataki noodles (1 package [198 g]) = 0 g protein | 5 g carbs | 0 g fat | 20 calories
- Spaghetti squash (1 cup cooked [100 g]) = 1 g protein | 7 g carbs | 0 g fat | 27 calories
- Brioche buns (Signature Select®;1 bun [50 g]) = 5 g protein | 26 g carbs | 3.5 g fat | 150 calories

Instead of buns try:

- Pitas (Joseph's™ Bakery; 1 pita [37 g]) = 6 g protein | 9 g carbs | 1.5 g fat | 60 calories
- Lavash bread (Joseph's Bakery; ½ lavash [64 g]) = 6 g protein | 8 g carbs | 1.5 g fat | 60 calories
- Lettuce cups/buns (6 leaves [74 g]) = 1 g protein | 3 g carbs | 0 g fat | 13 calories
- Dark leafy greens mix (1 full container, 5 oz [142 g]) = 4 g protein | 6 g carbs | 0 g fat | 40 calories
- Portobello mushroom caps (1 cap [85 g]) = 3 g protein | 4 g carbs | 0 g fat | 22 calories
- Bell peppers (1 medium pepper [148 g]) = 1 g protein | 7 g carbs | 0 g fat | 31 calories
- Corn tortillas (Mission®; 1 tortilla [24 g]) = 2 g protein | 19 g carbs | 1 g fat | 90 calories
- Low-carb wraps (Tumaro's® White Wrap; 1 wrap [40 g]) = 5 g protein | 13 g carbs | 2 g fat | 60 calories
- Egg wraps (Egglife® Everything Bagel; 1 wrap [28 g]) = 6 g protein | 0 g carbs | 1 g fat | 35 calories

best ever BREAKFASTS

We've all heard that breakfast is the most important meal of the day. Every meal is important—but starting your day off with the right foods certainly helps you stay energized, focused and on track with your fitness goals. This chapter is filled with tasty, easy-to-make breakfast options that will do just that.

In this chapter, you'll find a collection of macro-friendly breakfast recipes that are perfect for anyone wanting to fuel their body with the right balance of nutrients. From savory to sweet, there's something for everyone, and they all are designed to keep you feeling satisfied throughout the morning without compromising on flavor or nutrition.

Whether you're following a low-carb, high-protein diet or just looking for healthier breakfast options, this chapter has got you covered. So, grab your apron and let's get cooking!

Cinnamon Apple French Toast Casserole

You won't believe how easy and delicious this breakfast casserole is. It's simple to throw together, is low in calories and makes huge servings. This is a must-make on holidays or any time guests visit. If you're making this for yourself for the week, try reheating it in the air fryer for five minutes to get a nice crispy outside and a soft inside. This is terrific with the frosting or with syrup, or you could even try it over Greek yogurt for added protein.

NUTRITION	MACROS PER SERVING	OTHER NUTRITION
Total Servings: 8	**Protein:** 23 g	**Cholesterol:** 88 mg, **Sodium:** 316 mg, **Potassium:** 167 mg, **Dietary Fiber:** 2 g, **Sugars:** 20 g
Serving Size: 1 slice (160 g) plus frosting	**Carbs:** 42 g	
Calories: 306	**Total Fat:** 5 g	

14 slices cinnamon raisin bread

3 eggs

½ cup (120 g) liquid egg whites

1 cup (95 g) vanilla protein powder (Optimum Nutrition®)

1 tbsp (10 g) brown sugar, unpacked

½ tsp ground cinnamon

1 cup (240 g) unsweetened vanilla almond milk

⅓ cup (80 g) fat-free half-and-half

1 tbsp (15 g) lite maple syrup

1 medium Fuji apple, cored and chopped small (215 g)

Cinnamon Frosting
½ cup (112 g) nonfat (0%) plain Greek yogurt

1 scoop (31 g) vanilla protein powder (Optimum Nutrition®)

2 tsp (10 g) fat-free half-and-half

1 tbsp (15 g) honey

¼ tsp ground cinnamon

For Serving (optional)
Powdered sugar or Swerve® confectioners' sugar substitute

Slice the bread into 1-inch (2.5-cm) pieces, leaving on the crust. Arrange the slices on the bottom of a large greased baking dish. I use a 9 × 13–inch (23 × 33–cm); if you use a smaller dish, your bake time may increase by 5 to 10 minutes.

In a large mixing bowl, combine the eggs, egg whites, protein powder, brown sugar, cinnamon, almond milk, half-and-half and syrup. Whisk it to combine. Be sure to whisk until you have very few clumps from the protein powder, though it is okay to have some.

Pour the egg mixture on top of the bread. Top it with the apples. Cover it with foil and place it in the refrigerator for at least 2 hours; overnight is preferred. This will allow the bread to soak up the eggs.

When you're ready to bake, preheat the oven to 350°F (175°C). Remove the foil from the baking dish. Place it in the oven and bake for 45 minutes until the egg mixture is cooked through and no longer runny.

While the casserole bakes, make your frosting by mixing the yogurt, protein powder, half-and-half, honey and cinnamon until you have a frosting-like texture. Place it in the refrigerator until you're ready to serve.

To serve, slice the casserole into eight equal pieces, and top each with 20 grams of frosting and confectioners' sugar (if using).

Cheesy Sausage Frittata

A frittata is a brunch's best friend. They are easy to throw together and serve a lot of people. By using preseasoned lean turkey sausage, you've got a ton of flavor with a minimal amount of effort. Work smarter, not harder, right? This recipe does just that. This is a great recipe to make for meal prep, and it's great for a post-workout meal because it's low calorie and high protein.

NUTRITION	MACROS PER SERVING	OTHER NUTRITION
Total Servings: 8	Protein: 15 g	Cholesterol: 38 mg, Sodium: 391 mg, Potassium: 122 mg, Dietary Fiber: 0 g, Sugars: 0 g
Serving Size: 1 slice	Carbs: 1 g	
Calories: 112	Total Fat: 5 g	

16 oz (454 g) Jennie-O® lean turkey sausage (see Note)

¼ cup (28 g) shredded low-moisture part-skim mozzarella cheese

16 oz (454 g) liquid egg whites

1 cup (55 g) arugula

½ cup (90 g) chopped cherry tomatoes

⅛ tsp salt, plus more to taste

⅛ tsp pepper, plus more to taste

2 tbsp (14 g) shredded Parmesan and Romano cheese blend

Preheat the oven to 375°F (190°C). In a cast-iron skillet over medium heat, brown the turkey sausage for 7 to 10 minutes, breaking it into small bite-size pieces while cooking, until cooked through and no longer pink.

Once the meat is cooked through, remove the skillet from the heat and top the sausage evenly with the mozzarella cheese. Add the liquid egg whites, sprinkle on the arugula and lay the tomatoes down with the cut side up. Season with salt and pepper.

Place the cast-iron skillet in the oven for 25 minutes until the eggs are no longer runny and the center is firm. Remove the skillet from the oven and top the frittata with the cheese blend. Place it back in the oven for 2 to 5 minutes to melt the cheese. Remove and slice it into eight equal slices, and season to taste with salt and pepper.

NOTE: When looking for lean ground turkey sausage, you're looking for the kind that is sold as a larger log.

Sunday Quiche

Does "homemade quiche crust" sound intimidating and make you want to run for the hills or, at the very least, skip the page? Fear not. This one is so easy you'll be wondering what took you so long to try it. This quick, easy crust is the perfect macro-friendly crust for a savory breakfast.

NUTRITION	MACROS PER SERVING	OTHER NUTRITION
Total Servings: 8	Protein: 19 g	Cholesterol: 58 mg, Sodium:
Serving Size: 1 slice	Carbs: 7 g	605 mg, Potassium: 275 mg,
Calories: 240	Total Fat: 14 g	Dietary Fiber: 2 g, Sugars: 2 g

Crust

1½ cups (150 g) almond flour, plus more for rolling

¼ cup (32 g) unflavored protein powder (see Notes)

2 tbsp (28 g) unsalted butter, melted

¼ tsp baking soda

1 egg

¼ tsp salt

Filling

16 oz (454 g) Jennie-O® lean turkey sausage (see Notes)

1 small red bell pepper, diced

1 small head broccoli, tops only, finely chopped (100 g)

1 cup (235 g) liquid egg whites

¼ cup (60 g) milk

Salt and pepper, to taste

½ cup (56 g) shredded low-moisture part-skim mozzarella cheese

Preheat the oven to 350°F (175°C) and grease a round 9-inch (23-cm) pie dish or tart pan.

To make the crust, in a large mixing bowl, mix the almond flour, protein powder, melted butter, baking soda, egg and salt until well combined.

Using extra flour, roll out the dough softly to create a large circle the size of your dish. It will be sticky, so rely on the flour to keep it from sticking to the rolling pin. Lay the dough on top of the greased dish and press the mixture into the bottom and up the sides of the dish. Bake the crust for 8 minutes, or until it is lightly golden.

While the crust is baking, make the filling. Heat a large nonstick skillet over medium-high heat. Add the sausage, crumble it with a spatula and cook for 5 minutes until browned. Add the bell pepper and broccoli and cook until the vegetables are tender. Drain any excess liquid.

In a large bowl, whisk together the egg whites and milk. Season the mixture with salt and pepper.

Once the crust is baked, add a few pokes with a fork to the bottom of the crust and spread the sausage-and-vegetable mixture over the bottom of the crust. Pour the egg white mixture over the top of the sausage and vegetables.

Sprinkle the top with the cheese and place the quiche in the preheated oven for 45 to 50 minutes, or until the filling is set and lightly golden. Let the quiche cool for a few minutes, then season it to taste with salt and pepper. Slice the quiche into eight equal slices.

NOTES: I like Bob's Red Mill® unflavored whey protein powder for baking savory dishes like this, since it adds 15 grams of protein. You can omit it, but avoid using anything flavored as it might change the flavor of your crust.

When looking for lean ground turkey sausage, you're looking for the kind that is sold as a larger log.

Easy Breakfast Hash

If you're looking for a delicious and satisfying way to start your day, this hearty hash is the perfect choice. Packed with flavorful sweet potatoes, nutritious turnips and savory herbs and spices, this dish is a perfect fusion of wholesome and tasty. It's easy to prepare, and it's also customizable to suit your taste buds, making it a versatile addition to your breakfast routine.

NUTRITION	MACROS PER SERVING	OTHER NUTRITION
Total Servings: 4	Protein: 17 g	Cholesterol: 51 mg, Sodium: 493 mg, Potassium: 779 mg, Dietary Fiber: 5 g, Sugars: 10 g
Serving Size: 250 grams	Carbs: 22 g	
Calories: 219	Total Fat: 8 g	

16 oz (454 g) Jennie-O® lean turkey sausage (see Note)

3 cloves garlic, minced

½ medium white onion, diced

1 medium turnip, chopped (300 g)

1 large sweet potato, chopped (400 g)

⅓ cup (80 g) water

3 green onions, chopped

Salt and pepper, to taste

Chopped fresh dill (optional)

In a large cast-iron skillet, cook the breakfast sausage over medium heat for 5 to 7 minutes until browned and crispy, breaking it up into small pieces as it cooks. Remove the sausage from the skillet with a slotted spoon, leaving all excess liquid in the pan. Set it aside.

In the same skillet, add the garlic, onion, turnip and sweet potato. Cook until the onion has softened and the sweet potato and turnip have a nice browning on the outside, 5 to 7 minutes, stirring occasionally. Don't be afraid to let them burn a little in the skillet.

Once browned, add the water to the skillet and cover the veggies. Cook, stirring occasionally for 5 to 7 minutes until the potato has softened. Add the cooked sausage back into the skillet and stir to combine.

Add the green onions, salt and pepper and dill (if using). Serve alone or paired with your favorite style of eggs.

NOTE: When looking for lean ground turkey sausage, you're looking for the kind that is sold as a larger log.

Breakfast Fajitas

I love creating an easy, toss-together, flavorful breakfast I can reheat throughout the week. These fajitas are just that. Eat them as a simple egg scramble, make them in small soft tacos or roll them up for a high-carb breakfast burrito.

NUTRITION	MACROS PER SERVING	OTHER NUTRITION
Total Servings: 4 **Serving Size:** 89 grams veggies, 160 grams eggs (see Note) **Calories:** 183	**Protein:** 20 g **Carbs:** 12 g **Total Fat:** 5 g	**Cholesterol:** 185 mg, **Sodium:** 841 mg, **Potassium:** 409 mg, **Dietary Fiber:** 3 g, **Sugars:** 6 g

1 red bell pepper, thinly sliced (186 g)

1 yellow bell pepper, thinly sliced (158 g)

1 green bell pepper, thinly sliced (113 g)

½ yellow onion, chopped (145 g)

1 tsp salt

1 tsp ground cumin

½ tsp chili powder

Fresh cracked pepper, to taste

4 eggs

16 oz (454 g) liquid egg whites

2 tbsp (30 g) low-fat milk

⅛ tsp salt, plus more to taste

⅛ tsp pepper, plus more to taste

Chopped fresh cilantro

Preheat the oven to 450°F (230°C). Spray a baking sheet with nonstick cooking spray.

Add the bell peppers, onion, salt, cumin, chili powder and pepper to the baking sheet. Place it in the oven and bake for 10 minutes.

In a small bowl, whisk together the eggs, egg whites, milk, salt and pepper. When the timer goes off for the peppers, spray a large skillet with nonstick spray and heat it over medium heat. Scramble the eggs in the preheated pan for about 5 minutes with a spoon or rubber spatula until the eggs are cooked and no longer runny.

Remove the veggies from the oven. Toss them with the prepared eggs for a fajita scramble, or keep the veggies separate from the prepared eggs for a "create your own fajita" bar. Serve with cilantro for topping.

NOTE: Nutritional facts are for the eggs and peppers only.

Chipotle Breakfast Sandwich

Low on time this week and craving a quick fast-food breakfast sandwich? This is even better. Prepare two of these sandwiches, wrap them and place them in the fridge. Then just reheat in the microwave and get on with your morning. They're packed with protein and flavor, and they'll give you the energy boost your morning needs.

NUTRITION	MACROS PER SERVING	OTHER NUTRITION
Total Servings: 2	Protein: 20 g	Cholesterol: 123 mg, Sodium:
Serving Size: 1 sandwich	Carbs: 26 g	517 mg, Potassium: 93 mg,
Calories: 241	Total Fat: 9 g	Dietary Fiber: 8 g, Sugars: 1 g

Breakfast Sandwich

2 light English muffins

2 slices turkey bacon, cut in half

1 large egg

1 large egg white or 46 g liquid egg whites

Small handful of spinach, chopped

2 thin-cut slices sharp Cheddar cheese

Chipotle Sauce

1 tbsp (15 g) nonfat (0%) plain Greek yogurt

1 tsp chile in adobo, liquid only

Juice of 1 lime wedge

⅛ tsp garlic powder

⅛ tsp ground cumin

Salt and pepper, to taste

Preheat a medium nonstick skillet over medium heat. Toast the split English muffins in a toaster and set them aside. Cook the turkey bacon in the skillet for about 5 minutes until crispy on both sides, then transfer it to a paper towel–lined plate to remove any excess grease.

Add the egg and egg white to a small mixing bowl. Whisk the eggs together with a fork to combine and break the yolk. Spray the pan with nonstick spray and pour the eggs into the hot pan.

Let the egg cook through in the circle of the pan like you would cook an omelet, moving the uncooked egg toward the outside edges to cook and breaking lines in the center to push the raw egg to the bottom to cook.

Once the egg is cooked in a large circle, top it with the spinach and fold it in half like an omelet. Slice the omelet in half so you have two cooked egg halves. Depending on the size of your pan, you may need to fold the egg in half again to fit it on top of the English muffin. Top each egg with the cheese, then place a lid on top to let the cheese melt for 1 to 2 minutes.

While the eggs cook, make the sauce. Mix the yogurt, adobo liquid, lime juice, garlic powder and cumin in a small bowl. Season to taste with salt and pepper. Spread the sauce, split between the two sandwiches, on the undersides of the tops of the English muffins.

Assemble the sandwich by placing the cooked egg on the bottom half of the muffin, top with two slices of turkey bacon and the adobo sauce, and place the English muffin top on top.

Low-Carb Chocolate Granola

Say hello to your new go-to breakfast snack. This melt-in-your-mouth granola is crunchy, chocolatey and perfect for mornings when you're craving something sweet. Enjoy it with your favorite milk as a chocolatey low-carb cereal—hello kids!—or atop yogurt and fruit as a parfait. Or be like me and eat it straight out of the jar and don't tell anyone you made it so you don't have to share.

NUTRITION	MACROS PER SERVING	OTHER NUTRITION
Total Servings: 10 **Serving Size:** 22 grams **Calories:** 121	**Protein:** 4 g **Carbs:** 12 g **Total Fat:** 6 g	**Cholesterol:** 4 mg, **Sodium:** 30 mg, **Potassium:** 64 mg, **Dietary Fiber:** 1 g, **Sugars:** 3 g

1 cup (80 g) old-fashioned oats

2 cups (34 g) puffed rice cereal

1 scoop (31 g) vanilla protein powder (Optimum Nutrition®)

1½ tbsp (13 g) cocoa powder

¼ cup (60 ml) coconut oil, melted

¼ cup (60 g) lite maple syrup

Preheat the oven to 350°F (175°C). Line a baking sheet with parchment paper.

Add the oats, rice cereal, protein powder and cocoa powder to a large bowl. Mix it to combine. Add the melted coconut oil and maple syrup to the dry mixture. Stir to combine and coat all of the oats and cereal so no dry powder remains.

Spread the granola on the lined baking sheet so there are no large clumps, leaving a lot of space between the granola pieces. This will help dry it out while baking.

Bake the granola for 15 minutes, remove the baking sheet and mix it up. Place it back in the oven for 2 to 4 minutes, checking every couple of minutes to ensure you do not burn the granola. Remove once it is dry and crumbly. Break the granola into chunks. Store the granola in an airtight container for up to 4 weeks.

Harvest Breakfast Bowls with Creamy Dijon Sauce

This recipe isn't just for breakfast. The sky's the limit with these bowls. Add a fried egg to make it breakfast friendly, barbecue chicken for a lunchtime bowl, or leftover steak for a heartier dinner. One bowl, so many options—though please note that additions will change your macros.

NUTRITION	MACROS PER SERVING	OTHER NUTRITION
Total Servings: 4	Protein: 11 g	Cholesterol: 1 mg, Sodium:
Serving Size: 1 bowl	Carbs: 47 g	330 mg, Potassium: 433 mg,
Calories: 273	Total Fat: 4 g	Dietary Fiber: 5 g, Sugars: 6 g

1 cup (180 g) dry quinoa, uncooked

2 cups (475 g) water

1 tsp olive oil

2 cloves garlic, minced

1 shallot, finely sliced

8 oz (226 g) Brussels sprouts, shredded

5 oz (142 g) carrots, finely sliced in rounds (about 2 medium)

½ tsp salt

Fresh cracked pepper, to taste

Creamy Dijon Sauce

3 tbsp (45 g) Dijon mustard

¼ cup (52 g) nonfat (0%) plain Greek yogurt

3 tbsp (45 g) lite maple syrup

1 tsp apple cider vinegar

Toppings

Fried egg

Scrambled egg whites

Red pepper flakes (optional)

Add the quinoa and water to a medium saucepan and bring it to a boil over high heat. Once boiling, reduce it to a simmer and cover. Let it cook for 15 to 20 minutes until the quinoa has soaked up all the water. Fluff it with a fork.

While the quinoa cooks, add the oil to a large pan over medium heat. Once warm, add the garlic and shallot and cook for 1 to 2 minutes, stirring until fragrant. Be careful not to burn the garlic. Add the Brussels sprouts and carrots to the pan and sauté for 7 to 10 minutes until the carrots are soft and everything is nicely browned. Season with the salt and pepper.

To make the sauce, mix the Dijon, yogurt, maple syrup and vinegar in a small bowl. Set it aside.

Assemble your bowls with about 105 grams of quinoa, 80 grams of Brussels hash and 35 grams of sauce. Top them with eggs and some red pepper flakes for an added bite, if you'd like.

Banana Cream Puff Pancakes

If banana cream pie and cream puffs had a baby, it would be these pancakes. The sweet banana, vanilla and silky cottage cheese feel like you're enjoying a cream-filled donut. The cottage cheese is undetectable and adds protein—and all you're left with is a decadent treat you feel good about eating.

NUTRITION	MACROS PER SERVING	OTHER NUTRITION
Total Servings: 10 **Serving Size:** 1 pancake (see Notes) **Calories:** 98	**Protein:** 9 g **Carbs:** 13 g **Total Fat:** 2 g	**Cholesterol:** 42 mg, **Sodium:** 185 mg, **Potassium:** 135 mg, **Dietary Fiber:** 1 g, **Sugars:** 5 g

2 eggs

1½ cups (330 g) low-fat cottage cheese (see Notes)

1 banana, mashed (100 g)

3 tbsp (45 g) lite pancake syrup

¾ cup (90 g) all-purpose flour

1 scoop (31 g) vanilla protein powder (see Notes)

½ tsp baking powder

¼ tsp salt

2 tbsp (30 g) low-fat milk

Optional Toppings (see Notes)

Pancake syrup

Fruit of choice

In a large bowl, whisk the eggs and cottage cheese until well combined. If you want extra smooth pancakes, blend the cottage cheese with an immersion blender prior to adding; this is not necessary but helps with the texture.

To the cottage cheese mixture, add the banana and syrup. Stir it to mix just enough to combine. Do not overmix. Add the flour, protein powder, baking powder, salt and milk to the bowl. Stir to combine, but do not overmix.

Spray a large pan with nonstick spray and heat over medium-low heat. Using a ¼-cup (60-ml) measuring cup, pour the pancake mixture onto the warm pan. Once the batter begins to bubble and the edges lift easily, flip with a spatula; cook for 2 to 3 minutes per side until cooked through. Repeat with the remaining batter. Serve the pancakes with your favorite syrup and fruit of choice.

NOTES: Nutrition facts do not include syrup or fruit.

Make these pancakes even fluffier by whipping the egg whites by themselves until they form peaks prior to adding the yolks and cottage cheese.

I like Optimum Nutrition Gold Standard® Whey Vanilla Ice Cream protein powder and PEScience® Gourmet Vanilla protein powder, as well as Nancy's® organic probiotic low-fat cottage cheese.

Lemon-Blueberry Baked Oatmeal

This is one of my husband's top three recipes of all time. Topped with lemon yogurt icing, he can—and does!—eat an entire pan in one sitting. No harm, no foul, because this one is a nutritional powerhouse with a good amount of protein. With its fruity and zesty fresh flavors, this is a great way to welcome spring and to get use out of that lemon tree. Just be prepared to not want to share!

NUTRITION	MACROS PER SERVING	OTHER NUTRITION
Total Servings: 8	**Protein:** 10 g	**Cholesterol:** 55 mg, **Sodium:** 132 mg, **Potassium:** 140 mg,
Serving Size: 1 serving plus icing	**Carbs:** 30 g	**Dietary Fiber:** 3 g, **Sugars:** 15 g
Calories: 182	**Total Fat:** 3 g	

Baked Oatmeal

2 cups (160 g) old-fashioned oats

1 scoop (31 g) vanilla protein powder

1 tsp baking powder

¼ tsp salt

1 cup (240 g) unsweetened vanilla almond milk or milk of choice

2 large eggs, lightly beaten

¼ cup (84 g) honey or lite maple syrup of choice

¼ cup (67 g) unsweetened applesauce

1 tbsp (6 g) fresh lemon zest

¼ cup (60 g) fresh lemon juice

1 tsp vanilla extract

1¼ cups (190 g) fresh or frozen blueberries (if using frozen, do not thaw), divided

Lemon Icing

½ cup (112 g) nonfat (0%) plain Greek yogurt, plus more for serving

1 scoop (31 g) vanilla protein powder (Optimum Nutrition®)

1 tbsp (15 g) honey, plus more for serving

2 tbsp (30 g) fresh lemon juice

2 tsp (10 g) fat-free half-and-half, plus more if needed

Toasted almonds, walnuts or pecans, for serving

Preheat the oven to 350°F (175°C). Grease an 8 × 8–inch (20 × 20–cm) baking dish or line it with parchment paper.

In a large mixing bowl, combine the oats, protein powder, baking powder and salt. Mix it well to combine.

In a separate bowl, whisk together the almond milk, eggs, honey, applesauce, lemon zest, lemon juice and vanilla. Pour the wet mixture into the dry mixture, and stir until fully combined. Gently fold in 1 cup (152 g) of the blueberries, being careful not to crush them. Set aside the remaining blueberries.

Pour the oatmeal mixture into the prepared baking dish. Spread it out evenly and sprinkle the blueberries on the top of the mixture. Bake for 45 minutes, or until the top is golden brown and a tooth-pick inserted into the center comes out mostly clean.

While the oatmeal bakes, make the lemon icing. Add the yogurt, protein powder, honey, lemon juice and half-and-half to a small mixing bowl. Whisk well until the mixture is thoroughly combined. If the icing is too thick, add a little more half-and-half or water to thin it out to the desired consistency.

Once the oatmeal is done, allow it to cool for 5 minutes before cutting into eight 105-gram portions. Serve it warm or at room temperature with 20 grams of icing on top. The oatmeal will keep its form as it cools, making it easy to cut and store for meal prep.

NOTE: You can also serve the oatmeal with an extra drizzle of honey or maple syrup, a dollop of Greek yogurt, and toasted almonds, walnuts or pecans for added crunch. Please note that these extra toppings are not included in the nutrition facts.

easy pasta

IN JUST 30 MINUTES

Who doesn't love a hot and filling bowl of noodley goodness? It's the ultimate comfort food, filling our stomachs and our souls at the same time. For those new to following a macro-friendly diet, pasta may seem forbidden. I am here to set the record straight: Counting macros does not mean you have to give up what you love. That's the beauty of it. Eat what you want, stay within daily macro limits and eat the pasta!

This chapter is a collection of craveable pasta recipes that can be whipped up in no time. And this is probably my favorite chapter of all because I love pasta! Whether you're looking for a classic tomato-based pasta or something creamy and decadent, I've got you covered with a variety of recipes that are high in protein, low in carbs and packed with fiber to keep you full and satisfied.

So boil some water and get ready to indulge in some mouthwatering pastas.

One-Pan Chicken Fajita Pasta

If you're pressed for time, this one-pan recipe never fails. It's creamy, and it's packed with a perfect blend of protein and spices. Even better, it's ready in less than 30 minutes. My kids love this recipe, and I have no doubt it will be a family favorite for you too.

NUTRITION	MACROS PER SERVING	OTHER NUTRITION
Total Servings: 6 **Serving Size:** 270 grams **Calories:** 362	**Protein:** 39 g **Carbs:** 32 g **Total Fat:** 9 g	**Cholesterol:** 93 mg, **Sodium:** 585.4 mg, **Potassium:** 1064 mg, **Dietary Fiber:** 5 g, **Sugars:** 5 g

Pasta

1½ lb (680 g) boneless, skinless chicken breast, sliced into strips

1 red bell pepper, thinly sliced (188 g)

1 yellow bell pepper, thinly sliced (165 g)

1 green bell pepper, thinly sliced (120 g)

½ yellow onion, thinly sliced (135 g)

Salt

8 oz (226 g) uncooked chick-pea penne (Banza™)

2½ cups (570 g) low-sodium chicken broth

½ cup (110 g) fat-free half-and-half

½ cup (56 g) shredded Mexican cheese blend

Fajita Seasoning

1 tsp salt

1 tsp onion powder

1 tsp garlic powder

2 tsp (5 g) smoked paprika

1½ tbsp (12 g) chili powder

1½ tbsp (11 g) ground cumin

¼ cup (60 g) water

For Serving (optional)

Chopped fresh cilantro

Guacamole

Avocado

Plain nonfat (0%) Greek yogurt

Spray a large pan with nonstick spray and place it over medium heat. Add the chicken and cook for about 10 minutes, flipping halfway, until cooked through and no longer pink. Remove it from the pan and set it aside, leaving the juices in the pan.

To the same pan, add the bell peppers and onion. Sprinkle them with salt. Sauté for about 5 minutes until the onion is translucent and the peppers begin to soften. Add the chicken back to the pan.

To make the fajita seasoning, mix the salt, onion powder, garlic powder, smoked paprika, chili powder and cumin in a small mixing bowl. Add water to the seasoning mixture to create a paste. Add the seasoning paste to the chicken-and-pepper mixture. Mix everything together to coat.

Add the uncooked penne and broth to the pan with the chicken and peppers. Using a spoon, push the penne to the bottom of the pan so that it can cook in the broth. Bring it to a rolling boil. Lower the heat to medium and cover. Simmer it for 12 to 14 minutes, stirring often to ensure the pasta cooks through evenly in the broth.

Once the pasta is soft, add the half-and-half and cheese. Stir everything to combine. Serve the pasta topped with optional cilantro and any fajita toppings such as guacamole or avocado. Or try Greek yogurt in place of sour cream for added protein, if you'd like.

NOTE: To lower the carbs, use half the amount of pasta and broth, or omit it completely.

Chipotle Chicken Pasta

This is the perfect choice for those craving a delicious fusion of smoky, spicy and creamy flavors in a single dish. Combining tender chicken, perfectly cooked pasta and a rich chipotle sauce, this recipe is sure to make you come back for more. To make this even higher in protein, substitute with chickpea pasta.

NUTRITION	MACROS PER SERVING	OTHER NUTRITION
Total Servings: 6	**Protein:** 37 g	**Cholesterol:** 74 mg, **Sodium:** 858 mg, **Potassium:** 982 mg, **Dietary Fiber:** 4 g, **Sugars:** 6 g
Serving Size: 320 grams	**Carbs:** 51 g	
Calories: 404	**Total Fat:** 6 g	

1 tsp olive oil

1½ lb (680 g) boneless, skinless chicken breast, chopped

Salt and pepper, to taste

3 cloves garlic, minced

1 medium red bell pepper, thinly sliced

1 large head broccoli, chopped small

15 oz (425 g) tomato sauce

½ tsp salt

Fresh cracked pepper, to taste

½ tsp ground cumin

½ tbsp (4 g) chipotle powder (see Note)

½ tsp smoked paprika

3 cups (705 g) low-sodium chicken broth

12 oz (340 g) uncooked orecchiette pasta

⅓ cup (80 g) fat-free half-and-half

For Serving

Chopped fresh parsley

Grated Parmesan cheese

Add the oil to a large pan with high sides and heat it over medium-high heat. Add the chicken to the hot pan and season it with salt and pepper. Cook the chicken for 5 to 7 minutes, stirring often until it is cooked through and no longer pink in the center. Remove the chicken from the pan and set it aside. Discard the liquid in the pan.

Lower the heat to medium and add the garlic, bell pepper and broccoli to the hot pan. Sauté for 3 to 5 minutes to soften. Add the tomato sauce, salt, pepper, cumin, chipotle powder and smoked paprika. Stir it together to combine.

Add the broth and the uncooked pasta to the pan. Mix everything together and push the pasta down to submerge it in the liquid. Place a lid over the pan without sealing it, to allow some air into the pan. Bring to a boil.

Once boiling, lower the heat to a steady low boil, keeping the lid halfway on, and cook for 11 to 12 minutes, stirring often, until the pasta is slightly al dente. Remove the lid and stir everything together well. Add the half-and-half to the dish and stir to combine. Serve topped with parsley and Parmesan cheese.

NOTE: For a milder flavor, use ½ to 1 teaspoon of chipotle powder.

Lazy Lasagna

This Oh Snap Macros reader favorite has made its rounds on social media, and it deserves all its glory. It's packed with lasagna flavors without the tedious layering and baking that goes into a true lasagna . . . hence calling it lazy lasagna! Loaded with protein and ready in a snap makes this hearty dish a perfect weeknight meal.

NUTRITION	MACROS PER SERVING	OTHER NUTRITION
Total Servings: 6	**Protein:** 31 g	**Cholesterol:** 49 mg, **Sodium:** 244 mg, **Potassium:** 389 mg, **Dietary Fiber:** 2 g, **Sugars:** 1 g
Serving Size: 320 grams	**Carbs:** 39 g	
Calories: 422	**Total Fat:** 15 g	

8 oz (226 g) uncooked rigatoni

1 lb (454 g) lean ground beef (96/4%)

1 small yellow onion, chopped (100 g)

1 tbsp (10 g) minced garlic

1 tsp salt

1 tsp pepper

1 tbsp (3 g) Italian seasoning

½ tsp dried basil

1 (32-oz [907-g]) jar tomato basil pasta sauce (Rao's brand)

½ cup (120 g) low-sodium beef broth

4 oz (113 g) shredded low-moisture part-skim mozzarella

4 oz (113 g) part-skim ricotta cheese

For Serving (optional)

Chopped fresh basil

Grated Parmesan cheese

Cook the pasta according to the package directions. While the pasta cooks, heat a large pan over medium heat and brown the ground beef while breaking it into bite-size pieces.

When the meat is almost completely cooked through, about 5 minutes, stir in the onion, garlic, salt, pepper, Italian seasoning and basil. Cook for 3 to 5 minutes until fragrant and the onion begins to soften.

Stir in the pasta sauce and broth to combine. Simmer it for 3 to 5 minutes while the pasta finishes cooking.

Once the pasta is cooked, drain it and add it to the pan with the meat sauce. Let everything simmer for 2 to 3 minutes to combine the flavors and evenly distribute the pasta in the dish.

Add the mozzarella and stir everything together until the cheese is fully melted. While the lasagna is still hot, add the ricotta cheese on top and slightly mix it throughout the dish. Top it with basil and Parmesan (if using).

Philly Cheesesteak Pasta Skillet

This is a twist on one of my most popular blog recipes, Philly Cheesesteak Stuffed Shells. It's loaded with ground beef, mushrooms, bell peppers and a delicious, velvety white cheese sauce. Toss on chopped jalapeños to really pack a punch. When it comes to this easy, macro-balanced weeknight recipe, plan for minimal leftovers because it's highly unlikely you'll have any.

NUTRITION	MACROS PER SERVING	OTHER NUTRITION
Total Servings: 8	**Protein:** 30 g	**Cholesterol:** 56 mg, **Sodium:** 719 mg, **Potassium:** 437 mg, **Dietary Fiber:** 4 g, **Sugars:** 9 g
Serving Size: 250 grams	**Carbs:** 31 g	
Calories: 368	**Total Fat:** 13 g	

8 oz (226 g) uncooked medium pasta shells

1 lb (454 g) lean ground beef (96/4%)

½ yellow onion, diced (120 g)

1 red bell pepper, diced (180 g)

1 green bell pepper, diced (150 g)

7½ oz (213 g) whole baby bella mushrooms, thinly sliced

1 tsp salt

½ tsp pepper

1 tsp smoked paprika

1 tsp chili powder

½ tsp garlic powder

½ tsp onion powder

Cheese Sauce

1½ cups (355 g) whole milk

½ tsp garlic powder

Pinch of salt and pepper

1 cup (112 g) shredded low-moisture part-skim mozzarella cheese

1 cup (112 g) shredded Parmesan cheese

6 slices provolone cheese, thinly sliced

Chopped fresh parsley, for topping

Preheat the oven to 400°F (200°C). Bring a large pot of water to a boil and cook the pasta according to the package directions.

Heat a large cast-iron skillet or oven-safe pan over medium heat and add the ground beef. Cook it for about 5 minutes, breaking it into small pieces, until no longer pink. When the beef is cooked through, add the onion, bell peppers and mushrooms. Mix everything together well.

Add the salt, pepper, smoked paprika, chili powder, garlic powder and onion powder directly to the meat mixture. Stir it well to combine. Cover and let it simmer over medium heat for 5 minutes while the pasta cooks. Stir it occasionally so the bottom doesn't burn and everything cooks evenly.

When the pasta is done cooking, drain and add it directly to the pan with the meat.

To make the cheese sauce, return the pot you cooked your pasta in to the stove over medium heat. Add the milk, garlic powder, salt and pepper, then bring it to a simmer. Be careful, as the milk will boil over quickly, so pay close attention. Once simmering, remove it from the heat. Add the mozzarella and Parmesan cheese a little at a time and mix everything together as it melts.

Once everything has melted, whisk until the sauce is completely smooth and begins to thicken slightly. Pour the sauce on top of the meat mixture. Mix everything together to coat the meat and pasta with the cheese sauce. Top it with provolone cheese and place the skillet in the oven for 12 to 15 minutes, or until the sauce is bubbly and the top has browned. Sprinkle with parsley.

Steak Fettuccine Alfredo

I've taken the creamy, dreamy Alfredo sauce that makes fettuccine Alfredo a classic Italian favorite and re-created it to make a lighter, but equally decadent, dish. Tender, juicy steak paired with a perfectly cooked mixture of zoodles and pasta to keep carbs low and volume high, tossed together in a delicately rich Alfredo sauce—this one will have you reaching for more and feeling good about it.

1 lb (454 g) petite sirloin steak

¼ cup (60 g) coconut aminos

2 tbsp (30 g) lime juice

2 medium zucchini, spiralized (245 g)

Salt

8 oz (226 g) uncooked chickpea linguine (Banza™)

Alfredo Sauce

1⅓ cup (350 ml) fat-free half-and-half

¼ cup (55 g) low-fat cottage cheese

2 tbsp (28 g) butter

2 cloves garlic, minced

2 tbsp (16 g) all-purpose flour

¼ cup (28 g) shredded Parmesan and Romano cheese blend

For Serving

Fresh cracked pepper, to taste

Chopped fresh parsley

Grated Parmesan cheese

Slice the steak into thin slices against the grain. Place it in a resealable bag or sealable container. Add the coconut aminos and lime juice to the bag. Marinate the steak in the refrigerator for at least 1 hour prior to cooking. This can also be prepped the night or morning before cooking.

Place the spiralized zucchini on a paper towel and sprinkle with salt to allow it to absorb the water from the zucchini. Cook the pasta according to the package directions.

When the pasta has about 5 minutes left, start cooking the steak and making your sauce. Heat two separate large pans over medium heat. In one pan, add the steak and cook to your desired doneness. I prefer medium, about 5 minutes total.

To make the sauce, use an immersion blender or blender to blend the half-and-half and cottage cheese until there are no clumps. In the second pan, melt the butter, add the garlic and stir until fragrant. Add the flour and mix to form a paste. Slowly add the half-and-half mixture to the paste while whisking. The sauce will begin to boil and thicken as you whisk for about 3 minutes.

Once the sauce has thickened, remove it from the heat and add the cheese. Whisk until the cheese has melted. Once melted, add the zucchini and drained cooked pasta to the sauce.

Remove the steak from the pan and place it on a separate plate. Add the drippings from the meat to the pasta and mix it together to combine.

In order to have the most accurate serving size for this dish, I recommend keeping the meat separate from the pasta. Serve topped with pepper, parsley and a sprinkle of Parmesan cheese.

Low-Carb Beef "Noodles"

Say good-bye to takeout. After you try this heavenly interpretation of pad Thai, you'll have no need to order out. Heavy on protein and low on carbs, this dish satiates without putting you into a food coma. It travels great, reheats well and will leave you feeling energized and light. Sweet and salty perfection, this is a must for anyone looking for an alternative to a traditional carb-heavy pad Thai.

NUTRITION	MACROS PER SERVING	OTHER NUTRITION
Total Servings: 4	Protein: 33 g	Cholesterol: 162 mg, Sodium: 748 mg, Potassium: 515 mg, Dietary Fiber: 3 g, Sugars: 20 g
Serving Size: 280 grams	Carbs: 26 g	
Calories: 337	Total Fat: 11 g	

Beef "Noodles"

3 medium zucchini, spiralized (298 g)

Salt

3 large carrots (peeled into noodles, 255 g)

1 lb (454 g) lean ground beef (96/4%)

2 tbsp (30 g) water

2 eggs

3 green onions, chopped

1 tsp tapioca flour plus 2 tsp (10 g) water

Sauce

3 tbsp (45 g) fish sauce

3 tbsp (45 g) packed brown sugar

3 tbsp (45 g) rice vinegar

1½ tbsp (25 g) coconut aminos

1 tbsp (15 g) hot honey

1 tsp lime juice

For Serving

1 oz (28 g) peanuts, finely chopped

Red pepper flakes

Lay the spiralized zucchini on a paper towel and sprinkle it with salt to absorb the excess water while you prepare your dish. Peel the outside of the carrots and discard the skins. Continue peeling the carrots into long strips until you can no longer peel them. You should end up with a bowl full of carrot "noodles."

Heat a large pan over medium heat with nonstick cooking spray and add the ground beef. Using a wooden spoon or spatula, break the meat into small pieces. Cook through for about 5 minutes until no longer pink.

While the meat cooks, make the sauce. Add the fish sauce, brown sugar, vinegar, coconut aminos, hot honey and lime juice to a small jar with a lid. Cover it and shake it to combine. Set it aside.

Add the zucchini, carrots and water to the pan with the cooked meat. Cover and let it simmer for 3 to 5 minutes to soften the vegetables. Stir everything together to combine. Drain any excess liquid.

Push the meat-and-vegetable mixture to the sides and spray the center with nonstick spray. Add the eggs directly to the center and scramble. Once cooked through, stir in with the meat mixture. Add the sauce and green onions to the mixture. Mix everything together to coat the dish in the sauce. Let it simmer for 5 minutes to combine the flavors.

To thicken the sauce, make a small hole of just sauce in the pan by pushing everything aside. Add the tapioca slurry to the sauce opening, gently mix everything together and then stir to combine. Top with peanuts and serve with red pepper flakes for added spice.

Hawaiian Pineapple Shrimp Scampi

A whole lotta savory with a splash of sweet, this high-protein shrimp dish will be a staple in your weekly rotation. Light, buttery shrimp counterbalances the pasta topped with a touch of sweet pineapple. It's ready in minutes, but it tastes like it took hours. You'll want to make this week after week.

NUTRITION	MACROS PER SERVING	OTHER NUTRITION
Total Servings: 6	**Protein:** 21 g	**Cholesterol:** 186 mg, **Sodium:** 525 mg, **Potassium:** 232 mg, **Dietary Fiber:** 1 g, **Sugars:** 7 g
Serving Size: 137 grams (shrimp only)	**Carbs:** 10 g	
Calories: 163	**Total Fat:** 3 g	

2 lb (907 g) frozen jumbo shrimp 16–20 count, shells and tails removed (see Notes)

¼ cup (30 g) tapioca flour or cornstarch

1 tsp smoked paprika

2 tsp (10 g) olive oil

3 cloves garlic, minced

2 tbsp (30 g) coconut aminos or soy sauce

1 tbsp (15 g) pineapple juice

1 tbsp (15 g) fish sauce

1 cup (155 g) pineapple chunks

For Serving

Chopped fresh parsley

Fettuccine or zoodles (optional)

If using frozen shrimp, add the shrimp to a large bowl of lukewarm water to defrost. Do not use hot water, as this will cook the shrimp. Drain halfway through and add more water to continue to defrost. This takes roughly 10 to 20 minutes to thaw depending on how cold your water is.

In a resealable bag, add the tapioca flour, smoked paprika and raw shrimp. Shake to coat the shrimp with the flour mixture.

Add the oil to a large pan over medium heat. Add the garlic and sauté for 30 seconds to slightly brown. Be careful not to burn the garlic. Add the shrimp to the garlic oil and cook one side for 2 minutes. Flip with tongs and cook for 2 minutes, or until the shrimp is pink and no longer opaque.

While the shrimp cooks, mix the coconut aminos, pineapple juice and fish sauce in a small bowl. Add the sauce to the cooked shrimp, along with the pineapple chunks. Mix everything together to coat all the shrimp in the sauce.

Garnish with parsley. Serve with fettuccine or zoodles, or on its own.

NOTES: Purchasing deveined frozen shrimp with tails removed is your easiest, quickest option. Many frozen and fresh shrimp will have tails on and need to be deveined. Whichever you choose, opt for jumbo shrimp in the 16–20 range. Jumbo shrimp are important because they complement the pineapple well. Remember, once defrosted and without tails, the weight of the shrimp will change: 2 pounds (907 g) of frozen shrimp is equal to 1 pound 5.3 ounces (603 g) of fresh shrimp. Use this weight if substituting with fresh shrimp.

Hidden Veggie One-Pot Spaghetti

Want to fool the family into thinking you were in the kitchen all day preparing the ultimate family-friendly spaghetti? Look no farther. This dish requires one pot and is ready in less than 30 minutes. It also has hidden veggies for added fiber that I guarantee are undetected by toddlers and picky adults alike. Pair it with a side salad and freshly baked garlic bread for a quick and easy weeknight meal. Your secret is safe with me.

NUTRITION	MACROS PER SERVING	OTHER NUTRITION
Total Servings: 6	**Protein:** 31 g	**Cholesterol:** 47 mg, **Sodium:** 692 mg, **Potassium:** 401 mg, **Dietary Fiber:** 10 g, **Sugars:** 8 g
Serving Size: 330 grams	**Carbs:** 45 g	
Calories: 314	**Total Fat:** 2 g	

1 tsp olive oil

½ yellow onion, finely chopped or grated (100 g)

3 cloves garlic, minced

1 lb (454 g) lean ground turkey (99/1%)

28 oz (794 g) crushed tomatoes in tomato puree

2 tbsp (32 g) tomato paste

1 medium zucchini, finely diced or shredded (200 g)

1 tsp dried oregano

1 tsp salt

½ tsp dried thyme

½ tsp dried rosemary

Fresh cracked pepper, to taste

2 tsp (10 g) Worcestershire sauce

Red pepper flakes, to taste

2½ cups (570 g) low-sodium beef broth

10 oz (283 g) uncooked spaghetti (Barilla® Protein Plus; see Notes)

Heat the oil in a large pan with tall sides over medium heat. Add the onion and garlic. Sauté for 1 minute until the garlic is fragrant. Add the turkey and use a spatula to break the turkey into small pieces. Cook for 3 to 5 minutes, stirring often, until the turkey is cooked through and no longer pink.

Add the tomatoes in puree and tomato paste. Stir everything together to combine. Add the zucchini, oregano, salt, thyme, rosemary, pepper, Worcestershire sauce and red pepper flakes to the mixture. Stir to combine. Bring to a boil.

Once boiling, add the broth and uncooked pasta to the dish and submerge the pasta in the liquid. If your pan isn't as wide as the pasta, hold the pasta until it starts to soften at one end and slowly works its way into the dish, or simply break the pasta in half. Slightly cover the dish with a lid to keep the splattering contained; you still want air to get into the dish so do not seal the lid. I use a lid that is bigger than the pan.

Cook the pasta submerged in the sauce for about 8 minutes until the pasta is just over al dente, stirring often so it doesn't stick to the bottom of the pan. Different types of pasta will require different boil times so check the package to see the estimated time for the pasta you choose.

Once cooked, stir the pasta throughout the dish and serve. The pasta will soften as it sits in the sauce and the sauce will continue to thicken as it sets.

NOTES: This recipe uses Barilla Protein Plus spaghetti, which has 10 grams of protein per serving (2 oz [57 g]). You can substitute with chickpea pasta that has a similar macro breakdown or make this with regular spaghetti. This dish works with any kind of noodle.

Chicken Potpie Pasta

Chicken potpie? Yes, please. Pasta? Yes, please. Chicken potpie pasta? Sign me up. Cold, wintry months call for hearty meals, and this one is the ultimate. It uses only one pan and comes together quickly, and it's a fantastic way to satisfy the craving for a homestyle meal without sacrificing too many calories or too much time.

NUTRITION	MACROS PER SERVING	OTHER NUTRITION
Total Servings: 10	**Protein:** 33 g	**Cholesterol:** 70 mg, **Sodium:** 114 mg, **Potassium:** 403 mg,
Serving Size: 251 grams	**Carbs:** 38 g	**Dietary Fiber:** 2 g, **Sugars:** 5 g
Calories: 347	**Total Fat:** 10 g	

2 tbsp (30 g) olive oil

1 small yellow onion, chopped (200 g)

2 cloves garlic, minced

2 lb (907 g) boneless, skinless chicken breasts, cut into ½-inch (1-cm) cubes

Salt and black pepper

½ tsp dried thyme

½ tsp dried parsley

¼ cup (32 g) all-purpose flour

3 cups (705 g) low-sodium chicken broth

1 cup (240 g) fat-free half-and-half

14 oz (397 g) uncooked rotini (Barilla® Protein Plus)

12 oz (340 g) frozen mixed vegetables (peas, carrots, corn and green beans)

½ cup (110 g) low-fat cottage cheese, blended until smooth

Chopped fresh parsley, for garnish

Hot sauce (optional)

In an extra large skillet or a Dutch oven, heat the oil over medium heat. Add the onion and cook for 3 to 4 minutes, or until softened. Add the garlic and cook for 1 minute, or until fragrant.

Add the chicken and season with salt and pepper. Cook for 5 to 6 minutes, or until the chicken is no longer pink on the outside.

Stir in the thyme and parsley, then sprinkle the flour over the chicken mixture. Cook it for 1 to 2 minutes, stirring constantly to ensure even cooking and distribution of the flour. Pour the broth and half-and-half into the skillet, stirring to combine and dissolve any flour lumps.

Add the pasta and increase the heat to bring the mixture to a boil. Press the pasta down as best you can to submerge it in the liquid for cooking. Reduce the heat, cover and simmer for 8 to 10 minutes, stirring occasionally, until the pasta is cooked and has absorbed most of the liquid. Stir in the mixed vegetables and cook for 2 to 3 minutes, or until the vegetables are heated through.

Remove the skillet from the heat. Stir in the blended cottage cheese until well combined. It should be without chunks and creamy. Taste and adjust the seasonings as needed. Sprinkle with parsley and hot sauce, if desired.

Extra Creamy One-Pot Ham and Pea Pasta

Ever look at your holiday leftovers and think, *what now?* Ponder no more, my friend, because this pasta will use up that extra holiday ham in no time. Chop it up into cubes and make this ridiculously easy pasta. I like to add peas, but feel free to add leftover green beans, carrots or your favorite veggies.

NUTRITION	MACROS PER SERVING	OTHER NUTRITION
Total Servings: 6	**Protein:** 28 g	**Cholesterol:** 7 mg, **Sodium:** 841 mg, **Potassium:** 376 mg, **Dietary Fiber:** 7 g, **Sugars:** 7 g
Serving Size: 250 grams	**Carbs:** 41 g	
Calories: 321	**Total Fat:** 7 g	

1 tsp olive oil

2 cloves garlic, minced

2 cups (300 g) diced cooked ham (see Note)

8 oz (226 g) uncooked chick-pea pasta shells (Banza™)

3 cups (705 g) low-sodium chicken broth

1 cup (220 g) low-fat cottage cheese

¼ cup (65 g) fat-free half-and-half

16 oz (454 g) frozen peas

1 tsp onion powder

¼ tsp dried rosemary

¼ tsp smoked paprika

⅛ tsp cayenne pepper

¼ cup (28 g) grated Parmesan cheese

Salt and pepper, to taste

In a large pot or Dutch oven, heat the oil over medium heat. Add the garlic and cook for 1 to 2 minutes until fragrant. Add the ham to the pot and cook for 3 to 4 minutes until it starts to brown. Add the pasta and broth, then stir everything well to combine.

Bring the mixture to a boil, then reduce the heat to a simmer. Cover and cook for 10 to 11 minutes, stirring occasionally, until the pasta is al dente and has absorbed most of the broth.

While the pasta is cooking, blend the cottage cheese and half-and-half in a blender or food processor until smooth. Set it aside.

When the pasta is cooked, add the frozen peas and the cottage cheese mixture to the pot. Stir it well to combine, ensuring the pasta is coated evenly with the creamy sauce. Add the onion powder, rosemary, smoked paprika, cayenne pepper and Parmesan cheese. Stir it together well to combine.

Bring the pasta to a simmer to ensure the cottage cheese and Parmesan melts completely and the peas are heated through. Taste and adjust the seasoning with salt and pepper, as needed.

NOTE: Use leftover holiday ham or buy a precooked ham in your deli section. This recipe is not for deli sandwich ham.

one-pan
WEEKNIGHT WINNERS

Ever have those days where the last thing you feel like doing is cooking? The takeout menus and delivery apps call your name—but as you reach for your phone, your macros and your wallet bring you back to reality? My friends, this chapter is for you.

These recipes are designed to be cooked using just one pan, meaning less cleanup and more relaxation time. They're packed with nutrition, leaving you feeling good about what you're eating without sacrificing flavor.

Perfect for meal planning, these one-pan wonders will have you tossing out takeout menus and deleting those apps in no time. From Macro-Friendly Instant Pot Chili (page 67) to Peanut Chicken Stir-Fry (page 68), this chapter has something for everyone. So, grab your favorite skillet, turn on the stove and get ready to whip up some delicious, nutritious, macro-friendly meals in no time!

Macro-Friendly Instant Pot Chili

Hands down, this is my family's favorite go-to chili. The leftovers get better each day. And it freezes well, so it can be made ahead of time and pulled out when you're ready for it, making it a terrific meal-prep staple. Perfect for a chilly day when you want to get cozy under a blanket, this warming chili will be savored all winter long. My favorite topping is Sweet Heat jalapeños from Mt. Olive®; they add the perfect amount of sweet spice to the dish!

NUTRITION	MACROS PER SERVING	OTHER NUTRITION
Total Servings: 10	**Protein:** 28 g	**Cholesterol:** 57 mg, **Sodium:** 443 mg, **Potassium:** 442 mg, **Dietary Fiber:** 6 g, **Sugars:** 5 g
Serving Size: 390 grams	**Carbs:** 22 g	
Calories: 241	**Total Fat:** 6 g	

1 clove garlic, minced

1 lb (454 g) lean ground beef (93/7%)

1 lb (454 g) lean ground turkey (99/1%)

½ medium yellow onion, chopped

2 medium bell peppers, chopped (1 green, 1 red)

2 (14-oz [397-g]) cans diced fire-roasted tomatoes, undrained

1 (6-oz [170-g]) can tomato paste

1 (4-oz [113-g]) can diced green chiles, undrained

1½ cups (360 g) low-sodium beef broth

1 (15½-oz [439-g]) can mixed beans in a mild chili sauce, undrained (Bush's® Best)

¼ cup (30 g) chili powder

1 tbsp (7 g) ground cumin

1 tsp salt

1 tsp pepper

For Serving

Sour cream or nonfat (0%) plain Greek yogurt

Shredded Cheddar cheese

Chopped red onions

Avocado

Sweet Heat jalapeños (Mt. Olive®)

Turn the Instant Pot® to sauté. Spray the bottom with nonstick spray to prevent the meat from sticking. Add the garlic and cook for 1 minute until fragrant. Add the ground beef and ground turkey to the pot and cook for about 5 minutes until browned but not fully cooked through.

While still in the sauté function, add the onion, bell peppers, tomatoes and their liquid, tomato paste, chiles and their liquid, broth, mixed beans and their liquid, chili powder, cumin, salt and pepper. Stir it together well. Put on the lid and set to pressure-cook for 30 minutes. You can let this self-release all the way or quick release.

Open the Instant Pot lid and give the chili a good stir to combine. Serve topped with sour cream or yogurt, cheese, onions, avocado and/or jalapeños. Please note that this will change the macros listed in the nutrition facts.

Peanut Chicken Stir-Fry

This sauce is almost too good to be true. If there was ever any doubt that peanut sauce and chicken is the most delicious combo, this recipe will clear that debate right up. Highly addictive, this sweet-and-salty harmony will dance on your taste buds. The low-fat sauce goes with just about anything, so feel free to make extra.

NUTRITION	MACROS PER SERVING	OTHER NUTRITION
Total Servings: 4	Protein: 38 g	Cholesterol: 82 mg, Sodium: 583 mg, Potassium: 899 mg, Dietary Fiber: 7 g, Sugars: 19 g
Serving Size: 250 grams (see Note)	Carbs: 28 g	
Calories: 348	Total Fat: 9 g	

Stir-Fry

1 lb (454 g) boneless, skinless chicken breast, chopped into ½-inch (1-cm) cubes

Salt and pepper, to taste

½ head broccoli, chopped into bite-size pieces (135 g)

1 red bell pepper, thinly sliced (145 g)

½ cup (55 g) shredded carrots

3 oz (85 g) snow peas

2 green onions, chopped

2 tbsp (14 g) chopped peanuts

Peanut Sauce

1 cup (78 g) powdered peanut butter (PB2®)

½ cup (120 g) water

⅛ tsp ground cinnamon

2 tbsp (30 g) lite pancake syrup

¼ cup (75 g) coconut aminos

3 tbsp (45 g) red curry paste

2 cloves garlic, minced

¼ tsp red pepper flakes

Toppings (optional)

Chopped green onions

Chopped peanuts

Red pepper flakes

Serving Suggestions (optional)

Cauliflower, white or brown rice

Zoodles or Thai noodles

Lettuce wraps

Spray a large pan with nonstick cooking spray and heat over medium heat. Add the chicken to the pan and season it with salt and pepper. Cook it for 5 to 7 minutes until cooked through and no longer pink. Flip the chicken often so it cooks evenly throughout.

While the chicken cooks, add the broccoli to a medium microwave-safe bowl. Fill the bowl with enough water to slightly cover the bottom and microwave for 60 seconds to soften the broccoli.

To make the sauce, in a small bowl, mix the powdered peanut butter, water and cinnamon until you form a nice creamy peanut butter without any chunks. Add the syrup, coconut aminos, curry paste, garlic and red pepper flakes to the bowl. Mix it together well to combine and set it aside.

Once the chicken is cooked through, add the softened broccoli, bell pepper, carrots and snow peas to the pan. Mix everything together and cook it over medium heat for 5 minutes, stirring occasionally to soften the vegetables.

Once the bell pepper is fork-tender and slightly browned, turn the heat to low and add the peanut sauce to the mixture. Mix everything together to thoroughly combine. Top it with green onions, peanuts and red pepper flakes, if you'd like.

Serve the stir-fry over cauliflower rice, white or brown rice, zoodles or Thai noodles, or enjoy the stir-fry in lettuce wraps.

NOTE: Nutrition facts are for the chicken stir-fry only. You will need to include your rice, pasta or other sides you serve with this dish (see Sides and Volume Adds [page 18] for help with this).

Sausage and "Rice" Skillet

This skillet swaps out traditional rice for cauliflower rice to save carbs without sacrificing taste or texture! The savory flavors of the sausage combine with the delightful crunch and subtle nuttiness of the cauliflower rice. Cooked to perfection in a single skillet, this dish will have you singing from the rooftops about this swap. Be sure to make the homemade Cajun seasoning to use in other recipes!

NUTRITION	MACROS PER SERVING	OTHER NUTRITION
Total Servings: 4	**Protein:** 18 g	**Cholesterol:** 60 mg, **Sodium:** 1376 mg, **Potassium:** 453 mg, **Dietary Fiber:** 5 g, **Sugars:** 6 g
Serving Size: 291 grams	**Carbs:** 15 g	
Calories: 181	**Total Fat:** 6 g	

1 tsp olive oil

1 medium yellow onion, chopped

2 medium bell peppers, chopped

2 cloves garlic, minced

1 large head broccoli florets, chopped small

¼ cup (60 g) water

Salt and pepper, to taste

12 oz (340 g) red pepper and garlic chicken sausage, sliced cooked links (see Note)

12 oz (340 g) frozen cauliflower rice, cooked

Chopped green onions, for serving

Cajun Seasoning

3 tbsp (21 g) smoked paprika

1½ tbsp (25 g) salt

2 tbsp (14 g) garlic powder

1 tbsp (7 g) onion powder

1 tbsp (3 g) dried oregano

1 tbsp (5 g) cayenne pepper

1 tsp freshly ground black pepper

Heat the oil in a large skillet over medium heat. Add the onion and sauté for about 5 minutes until softened. Add the bell peppers, garlic and broccoli to the skillet. Cook them for 3 minutes to brown. Add the water, cover and cook for 5 minutes to soften the vegetables.

To make the seasoning, in a small container or mason jar, combine the smoked paprika, salt, garlic powder, onion powder, oregano, cayenne pepper and black pepper. Mix it together to combine.

Remove the lid on the skillet and add salt and pepper to taste. Add 1 tablespoon (7 g) of the Cajun seasoning to the vegetables. Stir everything together to combine. Reserve the rest of the seasoning for another recipe. Add the sausages to the pan with the vegetables. Cook them for 3 to 5 minutes, stirring often, to warm through and brown.

Once browned, stir in the cauliflower rice and cook for 3 to 5 minutes until heated through. Season with salt and pepper to taste and serve topped with green onions.

NOTE: I used Open Nature® chicken sausage—roasted red pepper and garlic (four links)—for this recipe.

Dad's Jambalaya

Dad's Jambalaya is more than just a dish. It's a memory that brings me back to my childhood each time I make it. My dad worked for an oil refinery—the same one his dad worked for and that I eventually got my first job with. He would often take trips to New Orleans for training. It was during these trips that he learned to make jambalaya from a friend. Over the years he perfected it, and it was a common request in our house. Here I've added my Oh Snap Macros twist to keep it lower carbs and higher protein without sacrificing the authentic flavors I grew to love so much.

NUTRITION	MACROS PER SERVING	OTHER NUTRITION
Total Servings: 8	Protein: 41 g	Cholesterol: 120 mg, Sodium: 1,170 mg, Potassium: 407 mg, Dietary Fiber: 1 g, Sugars: 1 g
Serving Size: 250 grams	Carbs: 31 g	
Calories: 382	Total Fat: 10 g	

4 smoked sausage links, thinly sliced into rounds (see Notes)

1 tbsp (15 g) olive oil

1½ lb (680 g) boneless, skinless chicken breast, chopped into bite-size pieces

1 lb (454 g) boneless pork chops, chopped into bite-size pieces

6 green onions, chopped

½ medium red onion, chopped

2 tbsp (14 g) Cajun seasoning (page 113 or use Tony's Chachere's® Original Creole Seasoning)

1 tsp garlic powder

1 tsp salt

½ tsp dried dill

½ tsp red pepper flakes

1½ cups (355 g) water

1½ cups (267 g) uncooked basmati rice

10 oz (283 g) frozen cauliflower rice

Chopped fresh parsley

Heat a large high-rimmed pan over medium-high heat and add the sausages. Let the bottoms of the sausage brown for about 5 minutes. Add the oil, chicken and pork chops. Stir and cook for 5 minutes, or until cooked through. Add the green onions, red onion, Cajun seasoning, garlic powder, salt, dill and red pepper flakes. Stir everything together to coat.

Add the water and uncooked basmati rice to the pan and stir so the rice is fully submerged in the water. Bring it to a boil and reduce to low heat. Cover with a tight-fitting lid and let it simmer for 20 minutes over low heat until the liquid has evaporated and the rice is fully cooked. Do not remove the lid while cooking.

While the jambalaya simmers, cook the cauliflower rice according to the package directions. Once the jambalaya is done simmering, scrape the burnt rice from the bottom with a wooden spoon and mix it in with the jambalaya. Add the cooked cauliflower rice and mix everything together well to combine. Top it with parsley.

NOTES: You can use my Cajun seasoning mix for this or Tony Chachere's Original Creole Seasoning.

I like Open Nature Andouille sausage or an Italian sausage.

To lower the heat, omit the red pepper flakes.

Frozen savory-herb-blend riced cauliflower works great in this recipe too.

Blackened Salmon Fajitas

Living in Alaska, we spend most of our summer fishing for halibut, salmon and rockfish. I take salmon seriously—if it doesn't pass my taste and texture test, it doesn't get served. I created this recipe with the flavor profile of salmon in mind, and the result is a perfect blend of flavor and crunch without being overwhelming. This blackened salmon can also be made on its own and paired with rice and veggies for a completely different, yet equally satisfying, meal.

NUTRITION	MACROS PER SERVING	OTHER NUTRITION
Total Servings: 12 **Serving Size:** 1 taco **Calories:** 118	**Protein:** 10 g **Carbs:** 17 g **Total Fat:** 5 g	**Cholesterol:** 22 mg, **Sodium:** 589 mg, **Potassium:** 103 mg, **Dietary Fiber:** 10 g, **Sugars:** 4 g

Pineapple Salsa

1 (8-oz [226-g]) can pineapple chunks, drained (5½ oz [156 g] drained)

3 small vine-ripe tomatoes, chopped (280 g)

¼ cup (4 g) chopped fresh cilantro

½ lime, juiced

¼ medium red onion, finely sliced

½ tsp salt

Fajitas

1 medium red bell pepper, thinly sliced

1 medium orange bell pepper, thinly sliced

1 medium red onion, thinly sliced (reserve ¼ for salsa)

1 lb (454 g) fresh wild caught salmon fillets

12 low-carb street taco flour tortillas (Mission®)

Blackened Seasoning

1 tbsp (7 g) smoked paprika

1 tbsp (7 g) garlic powder

1 tsp salt

¼ tsp pepper

¼ tsp cayenne pepper

To make the pineapple salsa, mix the pineapple, tomatoes, cilantro, lime juice, onion and salt in a medium bowl until well combined. Place it in the refrigerator to marinate while you make the fajitas.

Preheat the oven to 450°F (230°C). Add the peppers and onion to a baking sheet. Spray the vegetables with cooking spray and bake them for 10 minutes until softened and browned.

To make the blackened seasoning, add the smoked paprika, garlic powder, salt, pepper and cayenne to a small bowl. Mix well, then pour the seasoning onto the salmon fillets. Pat in to cover all sides; you may end up with some excess seasoning but try to use it all.

Remove the vegetables from the oven and push them off to the sides of the baking sheet. Place the salmon in the center of the baking sheet, skin side down, and return it to the oven. Bake for 12 to 16 minutes until the salmon easily flakes with a fork and is no longer mushy and pink on the inside. The time will vary depending on the thickness of your salmon.

Remove the baking sheet from the oven. Soften the tortillas by wrapping them in a damp paper towel and microwaving for 10 to 15 seconds. For a more charcoaled tortilla flavor, brown over an open flame on the stove.

Top your tortilla with 1.3 ounces (37 g) of cooked salmon, 13 grams of vegetables and 40 grams of salsa.

Shrimp Fried Rice

I love how the coconut aminos in this dish add a perfect amount of sweet to a savory meal. This fried rice is a perfect meal-prep recipe as it reheats great and just gets better as it sits. Not feelin' like bringing shrimp into the office? Try it with ground or sliced chicken, beef or ground turkey. Just be sure to cook the meat to temperature first.

NUTRITION	MACROS PER SERVING	OTHER NUTRITION
Total Servings: 5	**Protein:** 39 g	**Cholesterol:** 299 mg, **Sodium:** 1499 mg, **Potassium:** 510 mg, **Dietary Fiber:** 3 g, **Sugars:** 11 g
Serving Size: 350 grams	**Carbs:** 36 g	
Calories: 365	**Total Fat:** 7 g	

2 lb (907 g) frozen jumbo shrimp 16–20 count, shells and tails removed

1 tbsp (15 g) toasted sesame oil, divided

2 tbsp (20 g) minced garlic, divided

10 oz (283 g) frozen cauliflower rice

1½ cups (245 g) cooked basmati rice or 1 (8½-oz [241-g]) bag basmati ready rice

16 oz (454 g) frozen mixed vegetable blend (carrots, corn, green peas and green beans), thawed

2 eggs

¼ cup (75 g) liquid egg whites

Salt and pepper, to taste

½ cup (145 g) coconut aminos

¼ tsp ground ginger

2 green onions, chopped (plus more for serving, optional)

Red pepper flakes, for garnish (optional)

If using frozen shrimp, add the shrimp to a large bowl of lukewarm water to defrost. Be sure not to use hot water so the shrimp do not cook while defrosting in the bowl. You will need to drain the water about halfway through and re-add to keep them defrosting. This takes roughly 10 to 20 minutes to thaw depending on how cold your water is.

Using a wok or large pan, heat ½ tablespoon (8 g) of sesame oil and 1 tablespoon (10 g) of garlic over medium heat. Add the thawed shrimp to the wok and cook on each side for 2 to 3 minutes until they are no longer translucent and are pink throughout. Once cooked, remove the shrimp from the wok and set them aside.

Prep the frozen cauliflower rice and basmati rice by microwaving according to the package directions. Set them aside. To thaw the veggies, place them in a medium bowl of warm water.

Heat the remaining oil and garlic in the wok. Once warm, add the basmati rice and spread it to cover the bottom of the wok. Let it simmer for 2 to 3 minutes to begin to crisp the rice. Add the cauliflower rice and vegetables. Stir everything to combine.

Using a spoon or rubber spatula, make a hole in the center of the rice by pushing the rice to the outer edges of the wok. Spray the wok with nonstick spray. Add the eggs and egg whites, and season with salt and pepper. Using the spatula, scramble the eggs in the center of the wok until cooked through.

Once cooked through, mix the eggs together with the rice and vegetables to combine. Add the coconut aminos and ginger to the wok and stir. Simmer the fried rice for 3 to 5 minutes to be sure the liquid combines with the rice. Add the shrimp back to the wok along with the green onions. Mix everything together well to combine.

Serve alone or topped with more green onions, if you prefer, and red pepper flakes for some spice.

Creamy Green Chicken Enchilada Soup

There is nothing more comforting than soup during the cold months. This is one of those soups you can make time and time again and never get tired of it. It gets better when eaten as leftovers, freezes well and warms you right up with a little kick of jalapeño. This recipe is low calorie, creamy and guaranteed to be a favorite.

NUTRITION	MACROS PER SERVING	OTHER NUTRITION
Total Servings: 8 **Serving Size:** 290 grams **Calories:** 285	**Protein:** 33 g **Carbs:** 21 g **Total Fat:** 7 g	**Cholesterol:** 89 mg, **Sodium:** 881 mg, **Potassium:** 735 mg, **Dietary Fiber:** 4 g, **Sugars:** 6 g

2 lb (907 g) boneless, skinless chicken breast

1 tsp olive oil

1 medium yellow onion, diced

3 cloves garlic, minced

1 small jalapeño, seeded and finely diced (optional)

1 tsp ground cumin

1 tsp dried oregano

4 cups (940 g) low-sodium chicken broth

1 (15-oz [425-g]) can white beans, drained and rinsed

1 (15-oz [425-g]) can corn, drained

1 (4-oz [113-g]) can diced green chiles

1 (10-oz [283-g]) can green enchilada sauce

½ cup (8 g) chopped fresh cilantro

½ cup (112 g) fat-free half-and-half

Salt and pepper, to taste

½ cup (56 g) shredded Monterey Jack cheese

For Topping (optional)

Chopped fresh cilantro

Sliced radish

Tortilla strips

Add the raw chicken to a large pot of water to cover the chicken completely. Bring it to a boil and boil for 15 to 20 minutes until the chicken is cooked through and no longer pink. Using two forks or a hand mixer, shred the chicken and set it aside.

Heat a large soup pot or Dutch oven over medium heat. Add the oil and let it heat up. Add the onion, and cook for 3 to 4 minutes until softened. Add the garlic and jalapeño (if using), and cook for 1 to 2 minutes until fragrant.

Stir in the cumin and oregano, coating the onion, garlic and jalapeño. Cook it for 1 minute. Pour in the broth and bring the mixture to a boil. Reduce the heat to medium-low and let it simmer for 5 minutes to allow the flavors to meld. While simmering, use a wooden spoon to scrape the bottom of the pot and release all the flavors into the broth.

Add the chicken, white beans, corn, chiles and enchilada sauce to the pot. Stir it well to combine. Allow the soup to simmer for 15 minutes, stirring occasionally. Stir in the cilantro and half-and-half. Taste the soup, and adjust the salt and pepper as needed. Let it cook for 5 minutes, allowing the flavors to blend and the soup to thicken slightly.

Remove the soup from the heat, and slowly stir in the cheese until completely melted and incorporated. Ladle the soup into bowls and serve with your choice of toppings, such as cilantro, radish and tortilla strips.

Mom's Chunky Beef Stew

During the process of writing this cookbook, I lost my Mom. The grief of losing her was unimaginable. She was my rock and biggest cheerleader. She was an excellent cook, and through her meals she made our home a safe space for friends and family to gather, eat and laugh. Her talent in the kitchen was incredible: Stew, beef stroganoff and herb-crusted lamb chops are among my favorites, and they will forever remind me of her. She could do it all, and she did. I miss her every single minute of my day, and having her comforting and filling stew recipe in this book (and in the homes of everyone else who makes it) keeps her alive and in a beautiful way, here to experience this huge accomplishment with me.

NUTRITION	MACROS PER SERVING	OTHER NUTRITION
Total Servings: 8 **Serving Size:** 340 grams **Calories:** 252	**Protein:** 27 g **Carbs:** 16 g **Total Fat:** 7 g	**Cholesterol:** 70 mg, **Sodium:** 1,008 mg, **Potassium:** 877 mg, **Dietary Fiber:** 5 g, **Sugars:** 7 g

Stew Mix

2 tbsp (14 g) onion powder

2 tbsp (14 g) smoked paprika

1 tbsp (7 g) celery seed

1 tbsp (5 g) dried basil

1 tbsp (18 g) salt

2 tsp (2 g) dried oregano

2 tsp (2 g) dried rosemary

½ tsp chipotle chili powder

Beef Stew

1 tbsp (15 g) olive oil

2 cloves garlic, minced

2 lb (907 g) stew meat, chopped

1 cup (240 g) red wine vinegar

2 cups (475 g) low-sodium beef broth

1 cup (240 g) water or extra beef broth

½ large yellow onion, chopped thick

2 ribs celery, chopped thick

1 lb (454 g) carrots, chopped thick

1 lb (454 g) rutabagas, peeled and cubed bite-size (about 2 rutabagas)

12 Brussels sprouts, quartered

½ tsp herbs de Provence

Salt and pepper, to taste

Tapioca flour plus 2 tsp (10 g) water (optional)

Chopped fresh parsley, for topping

Preheat the oven to 325°F (165°C). In a small bowl, mix the onion powder, smoked paprika, celery seed, basil, salt, oregano, rosemary and chipotle chili powder.

Heat the oil in a 6-quart (5.7-L) Dutch oven over medium-high heat. Once the oil is hot, add the garlic and sauté for 1 to 2 minutes until fragrant. Add the meat and sear it on all sides until browned. Drain the excess liquid into a measuring cup.

Mix the liquid from the meat with the vinegar, broth, water and stew mix. Add it to the seared meat along with the onion, celery, carrots, rutabagas, Brussels sprouts, herbs de Provence, salt and pepper. Mix everything together well to combine.

Cover the pot and place it in the oven for 2 hours without opening. Don't peek! Once done, remove it from the oven and stir everything together to combine. You should have a chunky stew with minimal liquid. You can leave as is or add a tapioca slurry to thicken the liquid a bit. Both versions are delicious. Top it with parsley to serve.

NOTE: This is one of those recipes that I highly recommend weighing to get the most accurate serving size. The amount of moisture can vary depending on the meat, the veggies and the bake time.

Creamy Mediterranean Halibut

Besides incredibly cold winters and beautiful scenery in Alaska, I am also spoiled with fresh fish. I have learned about and tried so many fish varieties I could give the Seattle fish market vendors a run for their money. I've developed a love for white fish in particular for its mild, buttery flavor. Light, creamy and salty, this Mediterranean halibut is a perfect blend of flavors.

NUTRITION	MACROS PER SERVING	OTHER NUTRITION
Total Servings: 4	**Protein:** 25 g	**Cholesterol:** 59 mg, **Sodium:** 108 mg, **Potassium:** 493 mg,
Serving Size: 1 fillet with sauce	**Carbs:** 5 g	**Dietary Fiber:** 0 g, **Sugars:** 2 g
Calories: 187	**Total Fat:** 8 g	

1 lb (454 g) halibut fillet, sliced into 4 equal fillets

Salt and black pepper, to taste

1 tbsp (15 g) olive oil

¼ small yellow onion, chopped

2 cloves garlic, minced

½ cup (75 g) cherry tomatoes, quartered (about 8 tomatoes)

¼ cup (45 g) sliced kalamata olives

¼ cup (15 g) chopped fresh parsley

¼ cup (12 g) chopped fresh basil

½ cup (120 g) fat-free half-and-half

2 oz (57 g) crumbled fat-free feta cheese

For Serving

Lemon wedges

Roasted vegetables (optional)

Roasted Garlic Cottage Mashed Potatoes (page 140, optional)

Side salad (optional)

Preheat the oven to 375°F (190°C). Season the halibut fillets with salt and pepper.

In a large skillet, heat the oil over medium heat. Add the onion and garlic and cook for about 3 minutes until softened. Add the tomatoes and kalamata olives to the skillet and stir to combine. Cook for 3 to 4 minutes until the tomatoes are slightly softened. Remove the skillet from the heat and stir in the parsley, basil and half-and-half.

Pour the creamy tomato mixture into a 9 × 13–inch (23 × 33–cm) baking dish. Place the seasoned halibut fillets on top of the tomato mixture in the baking dish. Sprinkle the crumbled feta cheese over the top of the halibut fillets.

Bake the halibut for 20 to 25 minutes, or until the fish is cooked through and the cheese is melted and golden brown. Broil for 2 to 3 minutes at the end if needed. Serve hot with lemon squeezed on top and your favorite side dishes, such as roasted vegetables, mashed potatoes and a side salad, if you'd like.

Big Mac Casserole

Tracking your macros but craving a classic American McDonald's Big Mac®? This might not "technically" be a one-pan meal, but it is an absolute fan favorite and I couldn't deprive this book of it. This Big Mac Casserole has all the McDonald's flavors, and it is ready in no time. With its well-balanced macros, it's a great addition to your weekly rotation; just add a toy and you've got yourself a happy meal.

NUTRITION	MACROS PER SERVING	OTHER NUTRITION
Total Servings: 6 Serving Size: 230 grams (including toppings) Calories: 338	Protein: 23 g Carbs: 23 g Total Fat: 17 g	Cholesterol: 60 mg, Sodium: 518 mg, Potassium: 531 mg, Dietary Fiber: 2 g, Sugars: 5 g

1 tsp olive oil

1 lb (454 g) skin-on russet potatoes, chopped small

¼ cup (60 g) water

½ tsp salt, plus more for seasoning

¼ tsp pepper, plus more for seasoning

1 lb (454 g) lean ground beef (96/4%)

½ medium white onion, chopped

½ tsp garlic powder

½ tsp onion powder

2 tsp (10 g) yellow mustard

1 cup (112 g) shredded Cheddar cheese

Big Mac Sauce

¼ cup (60 g) light mayonnaise

¼ cup (65 g) ketchup

¼ cup (36 g) dill pickle chips, chopped

1 tbsp (15 g) dill pickle juice

Toppings

Handful shredded iceberg lettuce

Handful chopped white onions

1 vine tomato, chopped

¼ cup (36 g) dill pickle chips

Preheat the oven to 375°F (190°C). Heat a large pan over medium heat on the stove and add the oil to the pan. Add the potatoes and water to the hot oil. Season the potatoes generously with salt and pepper and cook for 7 to 10 minutes, stirring often so you do not burn the bottoms, until they begin to soften. Once the potatoes have softened, place them in a baking dish.

In the same pan you cooked the potatoes in, add the ground beef and onion. Cook for 5 to 7 minutes until the beef is mostly cooked through and the onion has softened. Season it with salt and pepper, and add the garlic powder, onion powder and mustard. Stir it to combine well. Add the cooked beef mixture to the potatoes and mix it together.

Top the mixture with cheese and cover with foil. Place it in the oven for 15 minutes until the cheese has melted.

While the casserole bakes, make the sauce. Combine the mayonnaise, ketchup, pickle chips and pickle juice in a small bowl. Stir to combine. Set it aside in the fridge.

When the casserole is done, remove it from the oven and remove the foil. Drizzle the sauce across the top—use it all! Top the casserole with lettuce, onions, tomatoes and pickle chips.

Cast-Iron Taco Pie

This dish is perfect for spicing up your Taco Tuesday routine! It combines the irresistible flavors of your favorite tacos with quiche and pie, all prepared in a trusty cast-iron skillet. Say good-bye to the mess of assembling individual tacos, and say hello to a new, delicious way to enjoy this classic Mexican-inspired low-carb favorite for any meal of the day.

NUTRITION	MACROS PER SERVING	OTHER NUTRITION
Total Servings: 8	Protein: 18 g	Cholesterol: 127 mg, Sodium: 473 mg, Potassium: 132 mg, Dietary Fiber: 2 g, Sugars: 3 g
Serving Size: 1 slice (135 grams)	Carbs: 6 g	
Calories: 147	Total Fat: 5 g	

1 lb (454 g) lean ground turkey (99/1%)

1 cup (7 oz [198 g]) cooked cauliflower rice

½ cup (95 g) canned corn, drained

½ cup (90 g) canned black beans, drained

½ cup (130 g) fire-roasted diced tomatoes

4 large eggs

½ cup (120 g) fat-free half-and-half

¼ cup (28 g) shredded Mexican cheese blend

Homemade Taco Seasoning

1 tsp salt

1 tsp onion powder

1 tsp garlic powder

2 tsp (5 g) smoked paprika

1 tbsp (8 g) chili powder

1½ tbsp (11 g) ground cumin

¼ cup (60 g) water

Toppings

Sour cream or nonfat (0%) plain Greek yogurt

Salsa

Chopped lettuce

Fresh cilantro leaves

Preheat the oven to 350°F (175°C). Heat a 9-inch (23-cm) cast-iron skillet over medium-high heat. Add the ground turkey to the skillet and cook it over medium heat, breaking it into smaller pieces as it cooks.

While the turkey cooks, cook the cauliflower rice according to the package directions. Add it to the cooked ground turkey.

To make the taco seasoning, mix the salt, onion powder, garlic powder, smoked paprika, chili powder and cumin in a small bowl. Add the water and mix to make a paste. Add the seasoning paste to the turkey and mix to coat. Add the corn, beans and tomatoes to the skillet. Stir it together to mix, then remove the skillet from the heat.

In a medium bowl, whisk together the eggs and half-and-half. Pour the egg mixture over the top of the meat mixture, making sure it's distributed evenly. Top it evenly with the cheese. Bake the taco pie for 20 to 25 minutes, or until the center is set and the edges are slightly golden.

Remove it from the oven and let it cool for 5 minutes. Cut it into eight equal slices and serve with your desired toppings.

bowls
AND HANDHELDS

If you're someone who loves to eat on the go or enjoys a comforting bowl of food, this chapter is perfect for you. I've compiled a collection of macro-friendly bowls and handheld recipes that are easy to make and packed with nutrients and flavor.

From chicken bowls to sandwiches to fiber-packed salads, these dishes are designed for people who want to fuel their body with the right balance of macronutrients without compromising on taste. Totally customizable to fit your personal preferences, these recipes are ideal for meal prepping and picky toddlers alike.

So, grab your favorite bowl and get ready to indulge in delicious, nutrient-dense macro-friendly meals that are perfect whether you're out and about or enjoying them from the comforts of home.

Blackened Chicken Salad

Chicken salad is delicious, this we know. I put this in sandwiches, wraps and salads, and honestly, I enjoy it right out of the mixing bowl, making it a perfect recipe for meal prepping. And this is no ordinary chicken salad—using chicken cooked with my homemade blackened seasoning really adds some pizzazz.

NUTRITION	MACROS PER SERVING	OTHER NUTRITION
Total Servings: 4	**Protein:** 30 g	**Cholesterol:** 87 mg, **Sodium:** 899 mg, **Potassium:** 553 mg, **Dietary Fiber:** 1 g, **Sugars:** 10 g
Serving Size: 190 grams	**Carbs:** 14 g	
Calories: 222	**Total Fat:** 5 g	

14 oz (397 g) cooked blackened chicken (page 122)

½ cup (50 g) finely chopped celery (2 ribs)

¼ cup (20 g) finely chopped red onion

⅓ cup (33 g) chopped shredded carrots

¾ cup (170 g) nonfat (0%) Greek yogurt

2 tbsp (30 g) Dijon mustard

2 tbsp (30 g) light mayonnaise

1 tbsp (21 g) honey

¼ tsp salt

Fresh cracked pepper, to taste

For Sandwich (optional)

2 slices of bread, bun, tortilla or pita of choice

Green leaf lettuce

Sliced fresh tomato

Cook the chicken according to the recipe directions on page 122.

Add the celery, onion and carrots to a large mixing bowl. Add the yogurt, Dijon, mayonnaise, honey, salt and pepper to the bowl. Mix it to combine well. Add it to the chicken and mix it together well to coat.

Serve on toasted bread with lettuce and fresh tomato, in lettuce cups, in wraps or just eat it straight out of the bowl.

Spicy Shrimp Tacos and Mango Slaw

There is something about fruit and fish together that is incredibly refreshing. This one combines sweet mango with shrimp and adds a touch of heat from chili powder to balance everything out. Served in warm tortillas, this meal packs a crunchy synergy of flavors while still being low fat and filling.

NUTRITION	MACROS PER SERVING	OTHER NUTRITION
Total Servings: 12	Protein: 11 g	Cholesterol: 93 mg, **Sodium:** 469 mg, **Potassium:** 63 mg, **Dietary Fiber:** 3 g, **Sugars:** 5 g
Serving Size: 1 taco with slaw	Carbs: 16 g	
Calories: 127	Total Fat: 2 g	

Mango Slaw

1⅓ cups (57 g) coleslaw mix

¼ cup (27 g) shredded carrots

3 green onions, chopped

¼ cup (40 g) chopped red onion

2 cups (350 g) chopped fresh or frozen mango

¼ cup (4 g) chopped fresh cilantro

2 tbsp (30 g) fresh lemon juice from ½ large lemon

Salt, to taste

Shrimp

2 lb (907 g) frozen tail-on large shrimp (31–40 count), defrosted, tails removed

1 tbsp (8 g) chili powder

½ tsp garlic powder

½ tsp smoked paprika

½ tsp salt

For Serving

12 corn tortillas

Butter lettuce leaves

To make the mango slaw, add the coleslaw mix, carrots, green onions, red onion, mango, cilantro, lemon juice and salt to a large bowl. Mix everything together and place it in the fridge to soak in the flavors while you prepare the shrimp.

Place the defrosted shrimp, chili powder, garlic powder, smoked paprika and salt in a large bowl, stirring to coat the shrimp.

Spray a large pan with nonstick cooking spray and heat over medium-high heat. Once hot, add the shrimp and cook for 2 to 3 minutes on each side until the shrimp is pink and no longer translucent. Remove the shrimp and set them aside.

Turn on a stove burner and brown the tortillas, warm them in the microwave or place them on a hot pan to heat prior to serving. Top each tortilla with butter lettuce, about 1.8 ounces (51 g) cooked shrimp and 38 grams of mango slaw.

Beef and Broccoli

I won't lie, I love takeout. What I don't love is the overly stuffed feeling that comes with it. Having a good copycat recipe for traditional takeout favorites gives you the best of both worlds, and this stir-fry does just that. Give this recipe a try the next time you feel like picking up the phone: It's nice and light. It has well-balanced macros, and it's ready faster than waiting on delivery.

NUTRITION	MACROS PER SERVING	OTHER NUTRITION
Total Servings: 6	**Protein:** 28 g	**Cholesterol:** 65 mg, **Sodium:** 318 mg, **Potassium:** 362 mg, **Dietary Fiber:** 3 g, **Sugars:** 6 g
Serving Size: 190 grams	**Carbs:** 12 g	
Calories: 213	**Total Fat:** 6 g	

3 tbsp (45 g) coconut aminos

1 tbsp (15 g) oyster sauce

1 tsp rice vinegar

1 tsp honey

¼ tsp arrowroot powder

¼ tsp ground ginger

¼ tsp red pepper flakes (plus more for serving, optional)

½ tbsp (8 g) olive oil

1½ lb (680 g) lean beef sirloin, thinly sliced

Salt and pepper, to taste

1 small yellow onion, thinly sliced (200 g)

2 cloves garlic, minced

6 cups (340 g) broccoli florets

¼ cup (60 g) water

Serving Suggestions

Cauliflower or basmati rice

Toasted sesame seeds (optional)

Dijon mustard (optional)

Chopped green onions (optional)

In a small bowl, whisk together the coconut aminos, oyster sauce, vinegar, honey, arrowroot powder, ginger and red pepper flakes. Set it aside.

Heat a large nonstick skillet or wok over medium-high heat. Add the oil, swirling to coat the surface. Add the beef to the skillet and season it with salt and pepper. Stir-fry for 3 to 4 minutes, or until browned but not fully cooked through. You still want the meat to be slightly pink and not overcooked. Remove the beef from the skillet and set it aside on a plate.

In the same skillet, add the onion and stir-fry for 2 minutes, or until softened. Add the garlic and cook for 30 seconds until fragrant. Add the broccoli florets and water to the skillet, cover and steam for 4 to 5 minutes, or until the broccoli is tender-crisp. Return the cooked beef to the skillet and mix it with the vegetables.

Pour the sauce over the beef and vegetables, stirring to coat evenly. Cook it for 1 to 2 minutes to allow the flavors to meld and the sauce to thicken. Taste and adjust the seasoning with salt, pepper and/or additional red pepper flakes for extra heat.

Remove the stir-fry from the heat and serve it immediately with steamed cauliflower rice or rice for a delicious bowl. Top it with toasted sesame seeds, Dijon mustard or green onions, if desired, though please note that these will change your macros slightly.

Jerk Chicken Bowls

We're going to Jamaica in a bowl with this one. Sweet, smoky and a little bit spicy, this jerk chicken seasoning will take your chicken to the next level. Serve it over rice with sweet mango and you'll have delicious, high-protein, meal-prep bowls all week long.

NUTRITION	MACROS PER SERVING	OTHER NUTRITION
Total Servings: 4	**Protein:** 39 g	**Cholesterol:** 110 mg, **Sodium:** 469 mg, **Potassium:** 650 mg, **Dietary Fiber:** 2 g, **Sugars:** 14 g
Serving Size: 1 bowl	**Carbs:** 39 g	
Calories: 359	**Total Fat:** 5 g	

Jerk Seasoning

1 tbsp (7 g) onion powder

1 tbsp (7 g) garlic powder

2 tsp (12 g) salt

2 tsp (3 g) dried thyme

2 tsp (9 g) sugar

1 tsp ground allspice

1 tsp smoked paprika

1 tsp cayenne pepper

½ tsp pepper

½ tsp dried parsley

½ tsp red pepper flakes

½ tsp ground cinnamon

¼ tsp ground cloves

¼ tsp ground cumin

⅛ tsp chipotle chili powder

Bowls

1½ lb (680 g) boneless, skinless chicken breast

1½ tbsp (10 g) jerk seasoning (recipe above or store-bought)

3 cups (420 g) frozen mangoes, thawed and chopped

⅓ cup (55 g) finely diced red onion

¼ cup (6 g) packed fresh cilantro, chopped

Pinch of salt

2 cups (326 g) cooked basmati rice

For Serving

Lime wedges

Chopped fresh cilantro

Heat a grill or indoor grill to medium-high heat. While the grill heats, make the jerk seasoning. In a small bowl, mix the onion powder, garlic powder, salt, thyme, sugar, allspice, smoked paprika, cayenne, pepper, parsley, red pepper flakes, cinnamon, cloves, cumin and chipotle chili powder. Set the jerk seasoning aside.

Using a meat pounder, pound the chicken to ½ inch (1 cm) thick. Using 1½ tablespoons (10 g) of jerk seasoning, season the chicken on all sides so that it's coated evenly. You will have plenty of seasoning left over for another use!

Spray the chicken with cooking spray to avoid sticking and place it on the grill on direct heat. Cook for 4 to 5 minutes on each side until the internal temperature is 165°F (74°C) and the chicken is no longer pink. The time will vary depending on the thickness of your chicken breasts. Remove the chicken from the grill and cut it into slices for your bowls.

Combine the mangoes, red onion, cilantro and salt in a large mixing bowl and set it aside. Assemble your four bowls with ½ cup (82 g) of cooked basmati rice. Top with 4½ ounces (128 g) of cooked chicken and 105 grams of mango salsa. Serve the bowls with limes to squeeze on top and some cilantro.

Creamy Blackberry Steak Salad

Don't get me wrong, I love a classic salad. However, eating the same ones over and over gets boring and makes us not want to eat salad at all. With that in mind, I give you this flavorful combo—I guarantee it's one you won't soon forget. The tender, juicy steak and tangy, tart blackberries come together with a creamy smooth dressing that will keep you wanting more.

NUTRITION	MACROS PER SERVING	OTHER NUTRITION
Total Servings: 4	Protein: 43 g	Cholesterol: 116 mg, Sodium: 355 mg, Potassium: 358 mg, Dietary Fiber: 5 g, Sugars: 10 g
Serving Size: 1 salad (see Notes)	Carbs: 17 g	
Calories: 368	Total Fat: 14 g	

Steak

1 lime, juiced

⅓ cup (80 g) coconut aminos

1 tsp toasted sesame oil

⅓ tsp garlic powder

1½ lb (680 g) flank steak

Creamy Blackberry Dressing

½ cup (112 g) nonfat (0%) plain Greek yogurt

1 cup (150 g) blackberries

1 tbsp (15 g) fresh lemon juice from 1 small lemon

1 tbsp (15 g) Dijon mustard

1 tbsp (15 g) red wine vinegar

1 tbsp (15 g) lite maple syrup

¼ tsp salt

Fresh cracked pepper, to taste

Assembly

5 oz (142 g) baby spinach and butter lettuce, mixed

½ medium cucumber, thinly sliced

½ cup (75 g) fresh blackberries

½ cup (75 g) fresh blueberries

2 oz (57 g) fat-free feta cheese, crumbled

To a sealable container or bag, add the lime juice, coconut aminos, sesame oil and garlic powder. Mix everything together. Add the whole flank steak to the bag and lay it flat in the fridge to marinate overnight. The longer the meat marinates, the more tender it will be (see Notes).

When you are ready to cook, preheat the grill to high heat (500°F [260°C]). Remove the marinated steak and place it on the hot grill directly over the flame. Cook it for 2 minutes on each side to get a good sear. Lower the heat to medium and cook for 3 to 4 minutes on each side until the center is to your liking. I prefer medium to medium-rare for salads, an internal temperature of 130°F (55°C). Remove the cooked steak from the grill and slice the meat against the grain into thin strips.

While the meat cooks, make the dressing. Add the yogurt, blackberries, lemon juice, Dijon, vinegar, syrup, salt and pepper to a high-speed blender or immersion blender cup. Blend until well combined.

Add the spinach and lettuce to a large bowl and top it with cucumber, berries, feta and the sliced steak. Pour the dressing over the top or serve it on the side.

NOTES: Each salad gets roughly 1¼ ounces (36 g) of salad mixture, 5 ounces (142 g) of steak and 80 grams of dressing.

If you do not have time to marinate for 24 hours, slice the steak into strips prior to adding to the marinade and marinate for at least 1 hour before cooking.

Grilled Blackened Chicken Caesar Cobb Salad

In this recipe, I've taken a chicken Caesar and introduced it to the Cobb, and the result is a fiery twist on two classics. Perfect for those who like their greens with a little extra spice, this creamy dressing delivers bright, tangy flavors atop seasoned blackened chicken and nutrient-packed greens. Perfect for meal prepping and customizable to your liking, this salad is sure to have you coming back for seconds.

NUTRITION	MACROS PER SERVING	OTHER NUTRITION
Total Servings: 4	**Protein:** 42 g	**Cholesterol:** 154 mg, **Sodium:** 1,145 mg, **Potassium:** 680 mg, **Dietary Fiber:** 2 g, **Sugars:** 3 g
Serving Size: 1 salad	**Carbs:** 9 g	
Calories: 330	**Total Fat:** 14 g	

Caesar Dressing

1 clove garlic, minced

¼ cup (60 g) fresh lemon juice from 1 large lemon

2 anchovy fillets, minced

1 tsp Dijon mustard

½ cup (112 g) nonfat (0%) plain Greek yogurt

1 tbsp (15 g) light mayonnaise

¼ cup (20 g) shredded Parmesan cheese

1 egg yolk

1 tbsp (15 g) water

Salt and black pepper, to taste

Assembly

1 lb (454 g) Blackened Chicken Breast (page 122)

2 heads romaine lettuce, chopped (365 g)

1 cup (150 g) cherry tomatoes, halved

¼ small red onion, finely sliced

2 hard-boiled eggs, sliced

¼ cup (28 g) shaved Parmesan cheese

5 slices turkey bacon, cooked and chopped

To make the dressing, in a small bowl, whisk together the garlic, lemon juice, anchovy fillets, Dijon, yogurt, mayonnaise, Parmesan, egg yolk, water, salt and pepper until well combined. Set it aside.

Cook the chicken according to blackened chicken directions on page 122. To assemble the salad, add the chicken, romaine, tomatoes, onion, hard-boiled eggs, Parmesan and bacon to a large mixing bowl. Mix it together to combine. Split into four equal salads and top each salad with 3½ ounces (99 g) of chicken and 40 grams of dressing.

NOTE: Use the Caesar dressing immediately, or store it in an airtight container in the refrigerator for up to 1 week.

Baked Salmon Poke Bowls

If you're in the mood for something light, fresh and bursting with flavor, a baked salmon poke bowl is just the ticket. A healthy, delicious twist on a traditional poke bowl, this one features baked salmon, a colorful array of veggies and a zesty Sriracha cream dressing. It's easy to prepare, perfect for lunch or dinner—and truly one of my favorite recipes.

NUTRITION

Total Servings: 2

Serving Size: 1 bowl

Calories: 382

MACROS PER SERVING

Protein: 34 g

Carbs: 18 g

Total Fat: 19 g

OTHER NUTRITION

Cholesterol: 64 mg, **Sodium:** 256 mg, **Potassium:** 1,185 mg, **Dietary Fiber:** 5 g, **Sugars:** 8 g

Poke Bowls

8 oz (226 g) wild salmon fillets

Salt and pepper, to taste

12 oz (340 g) frozen cauliflower rice

¼ medium cucumber, thinly sliced

2 large radishes, sliced

½ cup (55 g) shredded carrots

½ cup (75 g) shelled edamame

1 green onion, chopped

Sriracha Mayo

¼ cup (56 g) nonfat (0%) plain Greek yogurt

2 tbsp (30 g) light mayonnaise

1 tsp Sriracha, extra for spicy

½ tsp black sesame seeds

For Serving (optional)

Coconut aminos or soy sauce

Toasted sesame seeds

Preheat the oven to broil and line a baking sheet with foil. Cut the salmon into 1-inch (2.5-cm) chunks, leaving the skin on if your fillet has skin. If you're using skinless salmon fillets, spray the baking sheet with nonstick spray before laying the salmon chunks on top. If you're using fillets with the skin on, you can omit the nonstick spray as this will help to remove the meat from the skin.

Add the salmon to a large baking sheet and season it with salt and pepper. Place it in the oven and broil the salmon for 6 to 7 minutes until it is fully cooked, no longer mushy on the inside and easily flakes with a fork.

While the salmon cooks, make the Sriracha mayo. Mix the yogurt, mayonnaise, Sriracha and black sesame seeds in a small bowl. Set it aside.

Prepare the cauliflower rice in the microwave according to the package directions.

Remove the salmon from the oven. The skin should stick to the foil, allowing the meat to easily be removed. Add the salmon chunks to the Sriracha mayo. Mix them together to coat, being careful to not mix too hard as the salmon is soft and will flake apart easily.

Assemble your bowls. Add half of the cauliflower to a bowl with cucumber, radishes, carrots, edamame and half of the baked salmon mixture. Top with green onion and serve with coconut aminos or toasted sesame seeds (if using).

Buffalo Chicken Stuffed Peppers

I'm not sure what I love more about these stuffed peppers—the fact that they are simple and great to take on the go or the spicy, sweet-and-sour kick from the buffalo sauce. Topped with green onions, blue cheese crumbles and your favorite ranch dressing, you have a totally satisfying meal to bring to work or school. If you're a sauce gal like me, use a low-calorie ranch so you can get wild with it as opposed to limiting it to just a drizzle.

NUTRITION	MACROS PER SERVING	OTHER NUTRITION
Total Servings: 6 **Serving Size:** 1 stuffed pepper half **Calories:** 167	**Protein:** 21 g **Carbs:** 8 g **Total Fat:** 5 g	**Cholesterol:** 56 mg, **Sodium:** 871 mg, **Potassium:** 288 mg, **Dietary Fiber:** 4 g, **Sugars:** 5 g

1 lb (454 g) boneless, skinless chicken breast

¼ tsp garlic powder

Fresh cracked pepper, to taste

⅓ cup (80 g) hot sauce (Frank's RedHot®)

3 bell peppers, sliced in half lengthwise with core removed (red peppers are sweeter than green)

12 oz (340 g) frozen cauliflower rice, cooked and drained

¾ cup (84 g) shredded low-moisture part-skim mozzarella cheese

For Serving

Chopped green onions

Ranch dressing (not included in nutrition facts)

Tools

Instant Pot

Preheat the oven to 400°F (200°C).

Add the chicken, garlic powder, pepper and hot sauce to the bowl of the Instant Pot. Seal the lid. Set to pressure-cook for 8 to 10 minutes if using thawed chicken breast, or 18 to 20 minutes if using frozen.

While the chicken cooks, spray a 9 × 13–inch (23 × 33–cm) baking dish with nonstick spray. Add the bell peppers, cut side down, and spray the tops with cooking spray. Bake for 10 to 15 minutes to soften the peppers prior to adding the chicken. Broil at the end if needed to crisp the outside of the peppers.

Once the chicken is done, quick release and remove the lid from the Instant Pot. Shred the chicken with two forks in the bowl of the Instant Pot and mix it together with the liquid to coat the chicken.

Remove the bell peppers from the oven and add ¼ cup (50 g) of cooked cauliflower rice to the inside of each of the bell pepper halves. Top with 71 grams of cooked chicken and 14 grams of mozzarella cheese per pepper half.

Assemble each bell pepper half and bake them uncovered for 20 minutes until the cheese has melted and the bell peppers are soft. Top them with green onions and your favorite ranch dressing.

Spicy Chicken Tacos with Creamy Apple Slaw

I love tacos; there's no denying that. I love creating, making and eating tacos. What's not to love? They're an effortless thing to make on a busy weeknight, an easy vehicle for protein and you usually end up with leftovers to take for lunch the next day. If you weren't a taco lover before, you will be soon because you're going to love this sweet-and-spicy pairing.

NUTRITION - TACOS	MACROS PER SERVING	OTHER NUTRITION
Total Servings: 12	Protein: 11 g	Cholesterol: 19 mg, Sodium: 289 mg, Potassium: 108 mg, Dietary Fiber: 2 g, Sugars: 4 g
Serving Size: 1 taco	Carbs: 19 g	
Calories: 152	Total Fat: 3 g	

NUTRITION - SLAW	MACROS PER SERVING	OTHER NUTRITION
Serving Size: ¼ cup (40 g)	Protein: 1 g	Cholesterol: 1 mg, Sodium: 29 mg, Potassium: 48 mg, Dietary Fiber: 1 g, Sugars: 3 g
Calories: 24	Carbs: 5 g	
	Total Fat: 0 g	

Creamy Apple Slaw (see Notes)

2 cups (125 g) coleslaw mix

1 Fuji apple, cores removed and julienned (2 cups [180 g])

1 green apple, cores removed and julienned (2 cups [180 g])

4 green onions, chopped

½ lime, juiced

¾ cup (170 g) nonfat (0%) plain Greek yogurt

1 tbsp (15 g) Dijon mustard

2 tbsp (30 g) lite pancake syrup

1 tbsp (15 g) apple cider vinegar

½ tsp salt

Fresh cracked pepper, to taste

Tacos

1 lb (454 g) lean ground chicken (96/4%)

12 street taco–sized, flour tortillas

Chopped fresh cilantro, for garnish

To make the creamy apple slaw, in a large bowl, add the coleslaw mix, apples, green onions and lime juice. Mix everything well to combine.

To a mason jar or bowl, add the yogurt, Dijon, syrup, vinegar, salt and pepper. Mix it together or shake to combine. Pour the sauce on top of the coleslaw and mix it together well. Once combined, place the coleslaw in the fridge while you prepare the chicken.

Spray a large pan with nonstick spray, heat over medium heat on the stove and add the ground chicken. Break the chicken into small pieces and cook for about 5 minutes, stirring often, until the chicken is fully cooked and no longer pink.

(continued)

Spicy Chicken Tacos with Creamy Apple Slaw (continued)

Spicy Taco Seasoning

1 tbsp (8 g) chili powder

1 tbsp (7 g) garlic powder

½ tbsp (4 g) smoked paprika

½ tbsp (4 g) onion powder

1 tsp salt

½ tsp pepper

1 tsp red pepper flakes (half for mild spice)

5 tbsp (55 g) water

While the chicken cooks, make the spicy taco seasoning. Mix the chili powder, garlic powder, smoked paprika, onion powder, salt, pepper and red pepper flakes in a small bowl. Add the water to the bowl to form a paste. Add the seasoning paste to the cooked chicken. Mix it together to combine, then simmer it over low heat for 5 minutes to allow the chicken to soak up the flavors of the seasoning.

Using tongs and being careful not to burn them or yourself, brown the tortillas over the open flame of the stove. Alternatively, heat the tortillas in a hot pan or in the microwave to soften. Remove the chicken from the heat and the slaw from the fridge.

To make the tacos, top the tortillas with ¼ cup (40 grams or 1½ oz) of cooked chicken, ¼ cup (40 grams or 1½ oz) of creamy apple slaw and some cilantro.

NOTES: You can shred the apples if that is easier for you, but I prefer to julienne them by using a sharp knife and cutting them into long, thin strips. It helps keep the crunch of the apple. You will have leftover creamy apple slaw as it makes roughly 18 servings. Add it to wraps and sandwiches for some added crunch. Trust me, you'll want the leftovers. If the coleslaw is too thick, add a little water at a time to your desired consistency.

Grill
TO TABLE

Summer is the perfect time to fire up the grill and to enjoy delicious out-door cooking. You might think following a macro-friendly diet means your only option is bland barbecued chicken and rice. Fear not. In this chap-ter, I've compiled a collection of macro-friendly, grill-to-table recipes that are healthy, nutritious and easy to prepare.

From Blackened Chicken Breast (page 122) to Marinated Meat and Veg-gie Kabobs (page 114), these recipes are packed with protein, fiber and healthy fats to keep you feeling full and satisfied. They're also perfect for entertaining, so you can impress your friends and family with your delicious, healthy grill-to-table creations.

These recipes are easy to customize to fit your personal taste and prefer-ences, and the best part is that they can be prepared and cooked in no time. So, get your grill ready, stock up on your favorite macro-friendly ingredients, and prepare to enjoy some delicious, nutritious grill-to-table meals that are perfect for summer and beyond.

Cajun Shrimp and Sausage Kabobs

Nothing has a more Cajun feel than juicy shrimp, smoky sausage and rich savory spices. Barbecuing these kabobs results in a charcoaled blend of spices cooked into tender, juicy meat, giving you a taste of the bayou in your own backyard. Kabobs are one of my favorite ways to get in a ton of protein. Load them up, grill them and you've got endless protein for the week!

NUTRITION	MACROS PER SERVING	OTHER NUTRITION
Total Servings: 8	**Protein:** 23 g	**Cholesterol:** 118 mg, **Sodium:** 765 mg, **Potassium:** 0 mg, **Dietary Fiber:** 0 g, **Sugars:** 0 g
Serving Size: 1 skewer	**Carbs:** 1 g	
Calories: 130	**Total Fat:** 6 g	

Cajun Seasoning

3 tbsp (21 g) smoked paprika

1½ tbsp (25 g) salt

2 tbsp (14 g) garlic powder

1 tbsp (7 g) onion powder

1 tbsp (3 g) dried oregano

1 tbsp (5 g) cayenne pepper

1 tsp ground black pepper

Kabobs

1 lb (454 g) jumbo shrimp 32 count, peeled and deveined with tails removed

1 tsp olive oil

4 chicken sausage links (Italian or Andouille)

Tools

8 metal or wood skewers

For Serving

Chopped fresh parsley

Cooked white rice or cauliflower rice (optional)

To make the Cajun seasoning, mix the smoked paprika, salt, garlic powder, onion powder, oregano, cayenne and pepper in a small bowl.

In a medium mixing bowl, add the shrimp, oil and Cajun seasoning. Use 1 to 2 tablespoons (7 to 14 g) of seasoning based on the level of heat you want. Mix it together well to coat the shrimp. Save the remaining seasoning for another recipe.

Cut each sausage link in half and then into four to five rounds to place on the kabob with the shrimp.

Heat a grill or indoor grill pan over medium-high heat. Assemble the kabobs alternating shrimp and sausage. Each kabob gets four shrimp and half of one chicken sausage link.

Place the kabobs on direct heat and cook for 2 to 3 minutes on each side, or until the shrimp has fully cooked through and is no longer translucent and the kabob has a nice, browned sear.

Remove the kabobs from the heat, garnish them with parsley and serve immediately. Pair with rice or serve them alone.

Marinated Meat and Veggie Kabobs

Flank steak is my favorite red meat. It's lean, meaning lower fat, and it marinates beautifully, making it perfect for kabobs. Marinate this recipe overnight and the next day you have a meal-prep dream come true. This can be eaten in breakfast burritos, alongside rice, in a wrap or salad . . . the possibilities are endless! It comes together in 10 minutes after marinating by simply tossing it on the barbecue.

NUTRITION	MACROS PER SERVING	OTHER NUTRITION
Total Servings: 8	**Protein:** 19 g	**Cholesterol:** 56 mg, **Sodium:** 528 mg, **Potassium:** 125 mg, **Dietary Fiber:** 1 g, **Sugars:** 8 g
Serving Size: 1 skewer	**Carbs:** 11 g	
Calories: 192	**Total** Fat: 7 g	

Kabobs

1½ lb (680 g) flank steak

¼ cup (60 g) coconut aminos

1 tsp toasted sesame oil

½ tsp garlic powder

¼ tsp cayenne pepper

Skewers

8 metal or wood skewers

1 large green bell pepper, cut into 16 chunks

1 large red bell pepper, cut into 16 chunks

8 bella mushrooms, whole

½ large red onion, cut into 8 chunks

¼ cup (60 g) coconut aminos

Fresh cracked pepper, to taste

Chopped fresh parsley

Barbecue sauce

Slice the flank steak into strips, against the grain; you will fold these in half on the kabob as seen in the photo. Add the coconut aminos, oil, garlic powder and cayenne pepper to a resealable bag with the sliced meat. Move the meat around inside the bag so that the meat is submerged in the marinade. Place the meat in the refrigerator and marinate for at least 8 hours. Overnight is best and helps make the meat tender. I like to flip the bag in the fridge every few hours so all slices marinate nicely.

When you're ready to make your kabobs, heat a grill, indoor grill or grill pan over high heat and assemble your kabobs. Each kabob gets 3½ ounces (99 g) of marinated meat, two chunks of red bell pepper, two chunks of green bell pepper, one whole mushroom and one chunk of onion.

Assemble the kabobs and place them on a baking sheet with a rim to keep any juices from flowing over. Pour the remaining marinade and the coconut aminos over the tops of the kabobs and season with pepper.

Turn the heat to medium-high and place the kabobs directly on the grill over the heat. Cook them for 2 minutes on each side. Once you have cooked the kabobs for 4 minutes, move to indirect heat, cover the grill and let them sit for 2 to 5 minutes until you reach the desired doneness. The time will vary based on the thickness of your meat strips. For medium, I leave them on indirect heat for 2 minutes. Leaving the kabobs on indirect heat also helps the vegetables soften while the meat comes to temperature.

Remove the kabobs from the grill, sprinkle with parsley and serve with your favorite barbecue sauce for dipping.

Teriyaki Hawaiian Chicken Burgers

Give your chicken burgers a tropical twist. The sweet, tangy teriyaki sauce merges with grilled pineapple to create a melt-in-your-mouth barbecue chicken burger. No doubt your next barbecue will be one to remember with this mouthwatering, macro-balanced burger.

NUTRITION	MACROS PER SERVING	OTHER NUTRITION
Total Servings: 4 **Serving Size:** 1 assembled burger **Calories:** 407	**Protein:** 29 g **Carbs:** 40 g **Total Fat:** 13 g	**Cholesterol:** 110 mg, **Sodium:** 972 mg, **Potassium:** 156 mg, **Dietary Fiber:** 3 g, **Sugars:** 12 g

1 lb (454 g) lean ground chicken (96/4%)

¼ cup (26 g) almond flour

¼ cup (25 g) chopped green onions

1 slice canned or fresh pineapple, drained and chopped fine

1 tbsp (15 g) coconut aminos

½ tsp garlic powder

½ tsp salt

Fresh cracked pepper, to taste

4 slices of canned or fresh pineapple

4 lettuce leaves

4 brioche buns (150 calories each), toasted (see Note)

Sliced fresh tomato

Teriyaki Sauce

¼ cup (60 g) coconut aminos

½ tsp toasted sesame oil

½ tbsp (8 g) lite maple syrup

¼ tsp garlic powder

⅛ tsp ground ginger

¼ tsp tapioca flour

In a large mixing bowl, combine the ground chicken, almond flour, green onions, pineapple, coconut aminos, garlic powder, salt and pepper. Mix everything together well.

Form the mixture into four equal-sized burger patties, about 4.7 ounces (133 g) each. Using your thumb, press a hole into the top of each patty to prevent them from shrinking while cooking.

Preheat a grill or grill pan to medium-high heat. Grill the chicken burgers for 4 to 5 minutes per side, or until fully cooked through and the internal temperature is 165°F (74°C). When you flip the burgers, add the pineapple slices to the grill for the remainder of the time and grill both sides of the pineapple, flipping halfway through.

While the burgers cook, prepare the teriyaki sauce. In a small saucepan, whisk together the coconut aminos, oil, syrup, garlic powder, ginger and tapioca flour. Bring it to a boil. Simmer for 2 to 3 minutes to thicken.

Serve the burgers on a lettuce leaf or bun, topped with one slice of grilled pineapple, tomato and teriyaki sauce. Split the teriyaki sauce between four servings and use some drizzled on top and for dipping.

NOTE: To match the listed macros, use Signature Select® brioche hamburger buns at 150 calories (5 g protein | 26 g carbs | 3.5 g total fat) each.

Sun-Dried Tomato and Arugula Burgers

There is a time and place for a classic cheeseburger. This is not that time and not that place. The tartness of sun-dried tomato and tang of lemon fuses with peppery arugula to elevate a classic burger into something unique with a wild amount of protein. Even better, this recipe is easily doubled, making it a perfect addition to a summer cookout.

NUTRITION	MACROS PER SERVING	OTHER NUTRITION
Total Servings: 4 Serving Size: 1 burger Calories: 478	Protein: 52 g Carbs: 37 g Total Fat: 15 g	Cholesterol: 153 mg, Sodium: 1,183 mg, Potassium: 570 mg, Dietary Fiber: 3 g, Sugars: 7 g

Burgers

1 lb lean ground turkey (99/1%)

¼ cup (28 g) shredded Parmesan cheese

¼ cup (28 g) Italian-style bread crumbs

1 tbsp (15 g) finely chopped sun-dried tomatoes, without oil

2 cloves garlic, minced

¼ tsp dried oregano

1 tsp salt

¼ tsp dried thyme

1 egg

Fresh cracked pepper, to taste

4 slices low-moisture part-skim mozzarella cheese

Arugula Salad

1½ cups (90 g) packed arugula

½ tbsp (8 g) fresh lemon juice from 1 small lemon

½ tsp olive oil

Pinch of salt

Fresh cracked pepper, to taste

For Serving

4 brioche buns (150 calories each), toasted (see Notes)

4 slices tomato

Preheat a grill or grill pan to medium heat. In a large mixing bowl, make your patty meat by combining the ground turkey, Parmesan, bread crumbs, sun-dried tomatoes, garlic, oregano, salt, thyme, egg and pepper. Mix well until all the ingredients are evenly distributed, being sure to not overmix.

Divide the mixture into four equal portions about 5 ounces (142 g) each. Form the portions into four patties and use your thumb to press a hole in the center of each patty. This helps the patty to not shrink while grilling.

Spray the tops of the patties with nonstick spray to prevent them from sticking to the grill. Place the turkey patties on the grill and cook for 5 to 6 minutes on each side, or until the internal temperature is 165°F (74°C).

During the last minute of cooking, place a slice of fresh mozzarella cheese on top of each patty. Cover the grill or pan with a lid to help melt the cheese.

While the burgers are cooking, toast the hamburger buns until lightly browned. Make the arugula salad by combining the arugula, lemon juice, oil, salt and pepper in a medium bowl. Use your hands to massage the oil and lemon into the arugula to wilt it and shrink it down.

To assemble the burgers, top the bottom bun with tomato followed by the burger patty, arugula salad and top bun.

NOTES: To match the listed macros, use Signature Select® brioche hamburger buns at 150 calories (5 g protein | 26 g carbs | 3.5 g total fat) each.

To lower the calories, opt for a lettuce wrap, a burger salad or omitting the cheese.

Chicken Caesar Burgers

For a burger that's a little bit fancy and a lot delicious, try this chicken burger featuring homemade Caesar dressing. This recipe combines the juicy flavor of a chicken patty with the classic Caesar taste of homemade dressing, plus crisp lettuce and Parmesan cheese.

NUTRITION	MACROS PER SERVING	OTHER NUTRITION
Total Servings: 4	**Protein:** 36 g	**Cholesterol:** 75 mg, **Sodium:** 692 mg, **Potassium:** 136 mg, **Dietary Fiber:** 3 g, **Sugars:** 8 g
Serving Size: 1 assembled burger with dressing	**Carbs:** 34 g	
Calories: 395	**Total Fat:** 19 g	

Caesar Burgers

1 lb (454 g) lean ground chicken (96/4%)

1 egg

¼ cup (28 g) Italian-style bread crumbs

¼ cup (25 g) grated Parmesan cheese

2 cloves garlic, minced

1 tbsp (4 g) chopped fresh parsley

1 tbsp (15 g) Worcestershire sauce

1 tbsp (15 g) Dijon mustard

½ tsp salt

¼ tsp black pepper

Assembly

Leafy green lettuce leaves

4 brioche buns (150 calories each), toasted (see Note)

⅓ cup (80 g) Homemade Caesar dressing (page 100)

4 slices tomato

Sliced red onion

Preheat a grill or grill pan to medium heat. In a large mixing bowl, make the patty meat by combining the chicken, egg, bread crumbs, Parmesan, garlic, parsley, Worcestershire sauce, Dijon, salt and pepper. Mix well until all the ingredients are evenly distributed, being sure to not overmix.

Divide the mixture into four equal portions about 5.2 ounces (147 g) each. Form the portions into four patties and use your thumb to press a hole in the center of each patty. This helps the patty to not shrink while grilling.

Cook the chicken burgers for 4 to 5 minutes per side, or until the patties are fully cooked through to an internal temperature of 165°F (74°C) and are browned on the outside. Once the patties are cooked through, remove them from the grill.

To assemble the burgers, place a lettuce leaf on the bottom of each burger bun, a chicken patty on top of the lettuce, 20 grams of Caesar dressing and the tomato and onion. Top the burgers with the other half of the burger bun.

NOTE: To match the listed macros, use Signature Select® brioche hamburger buns at 150 calories (5 g protein | 26 g carbs | 3.5 g total fat) each.

Blackened Chicken Breast

This recipe is all about the seasoning. It's incredible. So incredible that I have this chicken in my fridge cooked and ready to go at all times—it's absolutely a macro-friendly meal-prep staple. I add it to just about everything: salads, wraps, bowls, you name it. It pairs well. Try it; you'll love it.

NUTRITION	MACROS PER SERVING	OTHER NUTRITION
Total Servings: 4	**Protein:** 26 g	**Cholesterol:** 83 mg, **Sodium:** 621 mg, **Potassium:** 406 mg,
Serving Size: 3½ ounces (99 g) cooked chicken	**Carbs:** 2 g	**Dietary Fiber:** 0 g, **Sugars:** 0 g
Calories: 137	**Total Fat:** 4 g	

1 lb (454 g) boneless, skinless chicken breast

Blackening Seasoning

1 tbsp (7 g) smoked paprika

1 tbsp (7 g) garlic powder

1 tsp salt

½ tsp pepper or fresh cracked pepper, to taste

⅛–½ tsp cayenne pepper (see Notes)

Heat the grill, indoor grill or grill pan to high heat. While the grill heats, trim the chicken breast, removing any fat.

Make the blackening seasoning by mixing the smoked paprika, garlic powder, salt, pepper and cayenne in a small bowl. Add it to the raw chicken. Be sure to cover all sides as well as you can with the seasoning. Spray one side of the chicken with cooking spray to prevent it from sticking to the grill.

Lower the grill to medium-high. Place the chicken on the grill with the nonstick coating side down, then close the lid and grill for 5 minutes. Flip the chicken and grill for another 5 minutes until it is cooked through or the internal temperature is 165°F (74°C). The time will vary depending on the thickness of the chicken breast. Once done, remove the chicken from the grill.

NOTES: Use the chicken for Blackened Chicken Salad (page 91) and Grilled Blackened Chicken Caesar Cobb Salad (page 100), or pair it with Roasted Garlic Cottage Mashed Potatoes (page 140), Air-Fryer Crispy Potato Wedges (page 139) and High-Protein Mac and Cheese (page 144).

Use ⅛ tsp of cayenne for mild heat, ¼ tsp for medium heat and ½ tsp for spicy.

Marinated Steak with Sweet-and-Spicy Chimichurri

I remember the first time I tried chimichurri. I was blown away by the flavors and with how well it paired with a perfectly grilled steak. The brightness of the herb-packed sauce was perfect with the richness of the meat. This extraordinary dish is a little bit sweet, a little bit spicy and a lot of absolutely delicious.

NUTRITION	MACROS PER SERVING	OTHER NUTRITION
Total Servings: 6 **Serving Size:** 4 ounces (113 g) cooked steak plus 30 g chimichurri **Calories:** 235	**Protein:** 24 g **Carbs:** 6 g **Total Fat:** 13 g	**Cholesterol:** 75 mg, **Sodium:** 66 mg, **Potassium:** 66 mg, **Dietary Fiber:** 0 g, **Sugars:** 5 g

Marinated Steak

¼ cup (60 g) coconut aminos

1 tbsp (15 g) fresh lemon juice from 1 small lemon

1 tbsp (15 g) fresh lime juice from 1 lime

1 tbsp (15 g) olive oil

1 tbsp (15 g) honey

3 cloves garlic, minced

1 tsp dried rosemary

Pinch of salt and pepper

2 lb (907 g) flank steak, whole not sliced

Sweet Heat Chimichurri Sauce

1 cup (60 g) packed fresh parsley

1 cup (20 g) packed fresh cilantro

3 tbsp (45 g) red wine vinegar

2 tbsp (30 g) honey

2 tbsp (30 g) olive oil

1 jalapeño, seeded and chopped

2 cloves garlic, minced

½ tsp kosher salt

Red pepper flakes, to taste

In a medium mixing bowl, whisk together the coconut aminos, lemon juice, lime juice, oil, honey, garlic, rosemary, salt and pepper. Place the flank steak in a large resealable bag and pour the marinade over the steak. Press out the excess air and seal the bag. Ensure the steak is well coated with the marinade by massaging the bag. Refrigerate for at least 2 hours, turning the bag occasionally. Overnight is always best to ensure a tender steak.

When you're ready to cook the steak, preheat the grill to medium-high heat, about 400°F (200°C). Make the sauce by adding the parsley, cilantro, vinegar, honey, oil, jalapeño, garlic, salt and red pepper flakes to a food processor. Pulse until the mixture is well combined and has a slightly chunky texture. Transfer the sauce to a small bowl and set it aside.

Remove the flank steak from the marinade and let excess marinade drip off. Discard the remaining marinade. Grill the steak for 5 to 6 minutes per side, or until it reaches your desired level of doneness. For medium-rare, aim for an internal temperature of 130° to 135°F (54° to 57°C).

Transfer the grilled steak to a cutting board, tent with foil and let it rest for 5 minutes. This will help the juices redistribute throughout the steak. Slice the steak thinly against the grain for maximum tenderness. Plate the flank steak, then drizzle it with sauce on top or serve the sauce on the side.

Grilled Steak Tacos

There can be no grilled section of this book without grilled steak tacos making the cut. Tacos are my go-to any time I am unsure what to cook for dinner, and these are incredible using your leftovers. Tender, flavorful meat is marinated for hours, then served with a warm tortilla, cabbage and queso fresco. It will turn your Taco Tuesday into a meal you want to make over and over again.

NUTRITION	MACROS PER SERVING	OTHER NUTRITION
Total Servings: 18 tacos	**Protein:** 13 g	**Cholesterol:** 38 mg, **Sodium:** 38 mg, **Potassium:** 71 mg, **Dietary Fiber:** 1 g, **Sugars:** 2 g
Serving Size: 1 taco	**Carbs:** 13 g	
Calories: 160	**Total Fat:** 7 g	

Cooked Marinated Flank Steak (page 99)

Sweet Heat Chimichurri Sauce (page 125)

½ cup (82 g) grilled corn on the cob

18 white corn tortillas, charred

1 cup (70 g) shredded green cabbage

1 cup (70 g) shredded red cabbage

½ cup (75 g) crumbled queso fresco

Cook the flank steak according to directions on page 99. Prepare the chimichurri according to directions on page 125.

For grilled corn, simply spray corn on the cob without the husks with cooking spray, season with salt and pepper and place on the grill while you cook the flank steak. They will take 10 to 15 minutes. Once they're properly charred, they "pop." This is when you pull them from the flame. Use a sharp knife and cut along the edges to remove the cooked corn from the cob and serve with your tacos.

Place the tortillas directly over an open flame on the stovetop and char both sides, using tongs to flip. Alternatively, soften the tortillas in the microwave.

Assemble your tacos using one tortilla, 1½ ounces (43 g) of cooked flank steak and 15 grams of chimichurri. Use this as your starting point as you add on your toppings such as cabbage, queso fresco and corn.

Honey-Garlic Shrimp Skewers

Honey, garlic and shrimp? Yes, please. These skewers are ridiculously easy to make, and they're flavor bombs that will have you reaching for seconds and thirds. The char on the shrimp from the barbecue is the perfect addition to the salty sweetness of the marinade and wonderful on its own, added to salad or with pasta.

NUTRITION	MACROS PER SERVING	OTHER NUTRITION
Total Servings: 6	**Protein:** 17 g	**Cholesterol:** 167 mg, **Sodium:** 873 mg, **Potassium:** 12 mg, **Dietary Fiber:** 0 g, **Sugars:** 8 g
Serving Size: 1 skewer or 6 jumbo shrimp	**Carbs:** 9 g	
Calories: 136	**Total Fat:** 3 g	

4 cloves garlic, minced

3 tbsp (50 g) honey (see Note)

3 tbsp (40 g) coconut aminos

1 tbsp (15 g) olive oil

½ tbsp (8 g) rice vinegar

Fresh cracked pepper, to taste

2 lb (907 g) frozen jumbo shrimp 16–20 count, shells and tails removed

Chopped fresh parsley, for serving

Tools

6 wooden skewers, soaked in water for at least 30 minutes or 6 metal skewers

Preheat a grill to medium-high heat. In a small mixing bowl, whisk together the garlic, honey, coconut aminos, oil, vinegar and pepper until well combined. Set aside a small amount for pouring on top of the shrimp at the end.

If using frozen shrimp, add the shrimp to a large bowl of lukewarm water to defrost. Do not use hot water, as this will cook the shrimp. Drain halfway through and add more water to continue to defrost. This takes roughly 10 to 20 minutes to thaw depending on how cold your water is.

Thread the shrimp on the skewers, piercing through both the tail and the head of each shrimp. For 2 pounds (907 g) of shrimp, each skewer gets six shrimp or about 4 ounces (113 g). Brush each skewer generously with the garlic-honey sauce, coating all sides of the shrimp.

Once the grill is hot, place the shrimp skewers on the grill and cook for 2 to 3 minutes per side, or until the shrimp turn pink and slightly charred. Brush the shrimp skewers with sauce before flipping them over. Be sure to reserve some sauce for serving.

Once the shrimp skewers are fully cooked, remove them from the grill. Serve the shrimp skewers with garlic-honey sauce poured on top and sprinkled with parsley.

NOTE: Use hot honey for a fun, spicy twist.

Peanut Chicken Skewers

When I first started counting macros, I was so disappointed to discover what a serving size of peanut butter actually looked like . . . eye-opening, right? Powdered peanut butter to the rescue, especially if you're in a calorie deficit. I guarantee you will not taste the difference in flavor in these skewers. We can have our peanut chicken . . . and eat it too. Serve the skewers over rice, vegetables, cauli rice or noodles—or serve alone as a fun party appetizer!

NUTRITION	MACROS PER SERVING	OTHER NUTRITION
Total Servings: 5	**Protein:** 38 g	**Cholesterol:** 99 mg, **Sodium:** 502 mg, **Potassium:** 674 mg, **Dietary Fiber:** 1 g, **Sugars:** 7 g
Serving Size: about 4.4 ounces (125 g) cooked chicken, plus dipping sauce split between 5 servings	**Carbs:** 12 g **Total Fat:** 5 g	
Calories: 263		

Peanut Sauce

1 cup (78 g) powdered peanut butter (PB2®)

½ cup (120 g) water

⅛ tsp ground cinnamon

2 tbsp (30 g) lite pancake syrup

¼ cup (75 g) coconut aminos

1 tbsp (15 g) red curry paste

2 cloves garlic, minced

¼ tsp red pepper flakes

Chicken Skewers

1½ lb (680 g) boneless, skinless chicken breasts, cut into 1-inch (2.5-cm) cubes or strips

Chopped fresh cilantro

Fresh lime wedges

Red pepper flakes (optional)

Tools

4–6 wooden skewers, soaked in water for at least 30 minutes or 4–6 metal skewers

In a large bowl, make the peanut sauce by mixing the powdered peanut butter, water and cinnamon to create a peanut butter consistency. Add the syrup, coconut aminos, curry paste, garlic and red pepper flakes. Mix it well to combine.

Place half of the sauce in a large bowl or resealable bag, saving the other half for dipping. Add the chicken pieces to the bag, ensuring they are fully coated in the marinade. Refrigerate for at least 30 minutes, or up to 4 hours for the best flavor.

Preheat a grill or grill pan to medium-high heat. Thread the marinated chicken onto the skewers.

Place the chicken skewers on the preheated grill or grill pan. Cook for 4 to 5 minutes per side, or until the chicken is fully cooked and the internal temperature is 165°F (74°C).

Drizzle the remaining peanut sauce over the skewers, or serve the sauce on the side for dipping. Garnish with cilantro, lime juice and red pepper flakes, if desired.

showstopping SIDES

A great side dish can elevate any meal to the next level. In this chapter, I've compiled a collection of showstopping sides that are macro friendly and packed with flavor and nutrients. From High-Protein Mac and Cheese (page 144) to Classic Coleslaw (page 135), these side dishes are designed to complement any main dish and to satisfy your taste buds. I've also included plenty of vegetable options, from Fancy Green Beans (page 147) to Loaded Cauli Mash (page 136), to ensure you're getting your daily dose of vitamins and minerals.

Whether you're looking for a comforting, indulgent side dish or a fresh and healthy one, this chapter has got you covered. These recipes are perfect for meal prep too, so you can prepare your sides in advance and enjoy them throughout the week. Grab your apron and get ready to wow your family and friends with some delicious, nutritious showstopping sides that are perfect for any macro-friendly meal.

Classic Coleslaw

For a healthier twist on a classic coleslaw, look no furthe; it has arrived. Crisp, crunchy salad, carrots and onions all tossed in a fresh, light dressing make a perfect side dish to your summer barbecue.

NUTRITION	MACROS PER SERVING	OTHER NUTRITION
Total Servings: 6 **Serving Size:** 120 grams **Calories:** 70	**Protein:** 5 g **Carbs:** 9 g **Total Fat:** 2 g	**Cholesterol:** 2 mg, **Sodium:** 127 mg, **Potassium:** 177 mg, **Dietary Fiber:** 2 g, **Sugars:** 6 g

Slaw

1 bunch green onions, chopped

2 cups (200 g) green cabbage, shredded

1 cup (100 g) red cabbage, shredded

1 cup (70 g) shredded carrots

Dressing

1 cup (224 g) nonfat (0%) plain Greek yogurt

2 tbsp (30 g) light mayonnaise

1 tbsp (15 g) lite pancake syrup

2 tbsp (30 g) apple cider vinegar

2 tsp (10 g) Dijon mustard

1 tsp celery seed

½ tsp poppy seeds

Salt and pepper, to taste

To a large bowl, add the green onions, cabbage and carrots. In a separate small bowl, make the dressing by combining the yogurt, mayonnaise, syrup, vinegar, Dijon, celery seed, poppy seeds, salt and pepper. Mix well until fully combined.

Pour the dressing on top of the cabbage mixture and mix thoroughly. Place it in the fridge in a sealed container for at least 30 minutes prior to serving to allow the flavors to combine.

Loaded Cauli Mash

I know what you're thinking: cottage cheese and cauliflower? Has she lost her mind? I assure you, I have not. Even my husband, who hates cauliflower, had three servings of this the first time I made it. The cottage cheese is packed with protein, and it creates a creamy mash when mixed with cooked cauliflower, cheese and turkey bacon bits. This mash feels every bit as decadent as its potato-and-butter counterpart. Serve it with your favorite chicken or steak, and prepare to amaze.

NUTRITION	MACROS PER SERVING	OTHER NUTRITION
Total Servings: 8	**Protein:** 15 g	**Cholesterol:** 35 mg, **Sodium:** 410 mg, **Potassium:** 367 mg, **Dietary Fiber:** 2 g, **Sugars:** 4 g
Serving Size: 160 grams	**Carbs:** 8 g	
Calories: 140	**Total Fat:** 6 g	

2 lb (907 g) cauliflower florets, cut into small pieces (about 2 heads)

10 pieces turkey bacon, cooked and chopped (10 oz [283 g]; see Notes)

1 cup (220 g) low-fat cottage cheese (see Notes)

½ cup (120 g) milk

¼ tsp garlic powder

Salt and pepper, to taste

½ cup (56 g) shredded Cheddar cheese

Chopped fresh chives

Add water to cover the bottom of a large pot. Add the cauliflower florets to the pot and bring the water to a boil. Once boiling, lower to a simmer and cook for 10 to 15 minutes until the cauliflower is fork-tender.

While the cauliflower is simmering, cook the turkey bacon in a large pan over medium heat for about 5 minutes until fully cooked through. Remove it from the pan and chop it into small bite-size pieces.

Drain the cauliflower and add it to a high-speed blender with the cottage cheese, milk, garlic powder, salt and pepper. Blend until smooth. Once smooth, add the cheese and blend until combined.

Remove the mashed cauliflower from the blender and place it in a large bowl. Mix in the cooked bacon and top the mash with chives. Add salt and pepper, if needed, and serve.

NOTES: I like Signature Select® turkey bacon, which is 45 calories per slice, and Nancy's® low-fat cottage cheese. Both Nancy's and Good Culture® are my go-tos when it comes to cottage cheese. Good cottage cheese makes a huge difference!

Air-Fryer Crispy Potato Wedges with Honey Mustard

It's a good thing potatoes are inexpensive because we go through bags of them in our house—partly because this recipe is in constant demand. The honey-mustard dipping sauce is the perfect addition to these simple, addicting potatoes. Get ready to leave your air fryer on the counter, because you'll be making these over and over again.

NUTRITION - POTATO WEDGES	MACROS PER SERVING	OTHER NUTRITION
Total Servings: 6 Serving Size: ⅙ of total cooked wedges (weigh for final serving size) Calories: 106	Protein: 2 g Carbs: 20 g Total Fat: 2 g	Cholesterol: 0 mg, Sodium: 380 mg, Potassium: 474 mg, Dietary Fiber: 2 g, Sugars: 1 g
NUTRITION - HONEY MUSTARD	MACROS PER SERVING	OTHER NUTRITION
Serving Size: 1 tbsp (25 g) Calories: 31	Protein: 2 g Carbs: 5 g Total Fat: 0 g	Cholesterol: 1 mg, Sodium: 64 mg, Potassium: 29 mg, Dietary Fiber: 0 g, Sugars: 5 g

1½ lb (680 g) potatoes (about 2 medium)

1 tbsp (15 g) olive oil

1 tsp garlic powder

1 tsp smoked paprika

1 tsp salt

Fresh cracked pepper, to taste

Chopped fresh parsley

Honey Mustard

½ cup (112 g) nonfat (0%) plain Greek yogurt

1 tbsp (15 g) yellow mustard

1 tbsp (15 g) Dijon mustard

½ tbsp (8 g) apple cider vinegar

2 tbsp (30 g) honey

Salt and pepper, to taste

Pinch of garlic powder, to taste

Tools

Air fryer

Preheat an air fryer to 400°F (200°C). Scrub the potatoes clean and cut them into wedges, about ½-inch (1-cm) thick.

In a large bowl, combine the potatoes, oil, garlic powder, smoked paprika, salt and pepper. Toss the potatoes to coat evenly. Arrange the potato wedges in a single layer in the air-fryer basket, making sure they are not touching each other. You may need to work in batches depending on the size of your basket.

Cook the potato wedges in the preheated air fryer for 15 minutes, flipping them halfway through the cooking time, until they are crispy and golden brown.

While the potatoes are cooking, make the honey mustard. Mix the yogurt, mustards, vinegar, honey, salt, pepper and garlic powder in a small bowl. Set it aside in the fridge until ready to serve.

Once the potato wedges are done, remove them from the basket and place on a serving plate. Sprinkle them with parsley and serve with the honey mustard.

NOTE: The honey mustard makes about 175 grams. I am providing the nutrition facts for 1 tablespoon (25 g) so that you can use your desired amount of sauce for dipping or using on burgers, wraps, salads and so on.

Roasted Garlic Cottage Mashed Potatoes

These mashed potatoes are the perfect side to bring to your next gathering. No one will know your secret ingredient is cottage cheese. I should know because I've made them 1,000 times and am repeatedly told how amazing they are. The roasted garlic is totally worth the bake time, adding a sweet and nutty flavor to the potatoes.

NUTRITION	MACROS PER SERVING	OTHER NUTRITION
Total Servings: 10	Protein: 4 g	Cholesterol: 7 mg, Sodium: 109 mg, Potassium: 607 mg, Dietary Fiber: 2 g, Sugars: 1 g
Serving Size: 150 grams	Carbs: 26 g	
Calories: 140	Total Fat: 3 g	

Mashed Potatoes

1 head raw garlic in skin (see Note)

1 tsp olive oil

3 lb (1.4 kg) sweet golden petite potatoes, skin on and quartered

3 green onions, chopped

2 tbsp (28 g) butter

Cream Sauce

½ cup (110 g) low-fat cottage cheese

2 tbsp (30 g) almond milk

¼ tsp salt, plus more to taste

Fresh cracked pepper, to taste

Preheat the oven to 400°F (200°C). Peel and discard the papery outer layers of the whole garlic bulb. Leave intact the skins of the individual cloves of garlic.

Using a sharp knife, cut ¼ to a ½ inch (6 mm to 1 cm) from the top of the head to expose the individual garlic cloves. Place the garlic on a piece of foil large enough to wrap around the entire head of garlic. Drizzle the oil on the top so that it seeps down into the garlic. Wrap the foil around the garlic, tenting at the top so it doesn't stick to the garlic while roasting. Place the foil-wrapped garlic on a baking sheet and roast for 60 to 70 minutes until the garlic starts to shoot out and can be easily squeezed out.

When the garlic has 10 minutes left, start prepping your potatoes. Place the potatoes in a pot with enough water to cover the top and bring it to a boil. Boil for 15 to 20 minutes until the potatoes are fork-tender for mashing.

Once the garlic is roasted, make the cream sauce. Remove the garlic from the oven and squeeze all the cloves into the cup of your immersion blender or a bowl. The garlic should squeeze out easily. Add the cottage cheese, almond milk, salt and pepper to the garlic. Blend until smooth.

Drain the potatoes and add them back to the large pot. Mash them with a potato masher or handheld mixer to make it extra smooth. Once no large chunks remain, add the cream sauce and continue mixing. Add the green onions and butter. Mix until smooth, then season with salt and pepper to taste.

NOTE: If you do not want to roast garlic, use 4 to 6 tablespoons (40 to 60 g) of fresh minced garlic to taste or 3½ tablespoons (25 g) of garlic powder in its place.

High-Protein Baked Beans

I grew up with baked beans and have loved them for as long as I can remember. Once I started counting macros, I knew I had to develop a baked bean recipe that reminded me of my childhood but was higher in protein. Let me tell you something, these are better. Protein-packed and reminiscent of the classic, these will be an absolute hit at the next potluck or barbecue.

NUTRITION	MACROS PER SERVING	OTHER NUTRITION
Total Servings: 8 **Serving Size:** 175 grams **Calories:** 197	**Protein:** 14 g **Carbs:** 28 g **Total Fat:** 4 g	**Cholesterol:** 25 mg, **Sodium:** 838 mg, **Potassium:** 649 mg, **Dietary Fiber:** 9 g, **Sugars:** 5 g

2 (15½-oz [439-g] each) cans navy beans, drained and rinsed

1 (15-oz [425-g]) can tomato sauce

¼ cup (60 g) lite pancake syrup

¼ cup (60 g) apple cider vinegar

½ small yellow onion, chopped (100 g)

1 medium red bell pepper, chopped

1 tsp garlic powder

1 tsp smoked paprika

½ tsp dried thyme

½ tsp dried rosemary

½ tsp chili powder

1 tsp dried oregano

Salt and pepper, to taste

16 oz (454 g) Jennie-O® lean ground turkey sausage (see Note)

Preheat the oven to 350°F (175°C).

In a large bowl, mix the navy beans, tomato sauce, syrup, vinegar, onion, bell pepper, garlic powder, smoked paprika, thyme, rosemary, chili powder and oregano until well combined. Season with salt and pepper.

In a pan over medium-high heat, cook the turkey sausage through for 5 to 7 minutes, crumbling it as it cooks, until no longer pink. Add the sausage to the bean mixture. Stir until well combined.

Pour the bean mixture into an 8 × 8–inch (20 × 20–cm) baking dish and bake the beans for 50 to 60 minutes, or until the mixture is hot and bubbly. Let the baked beans cool for 2 to 3 minutes before serving.

NOTE: When looking for lean ground turkey sausage, you're looking for the kind that is sold as a larger log.

High-Protein Mac and Cheese

Cozy, cold nights in our house call for classic comfort foods, with mac and cheese being a leading contender. This recipe results in a creamy, rich mac and cheese without the powdered packet of cheese. The undetectable noodle swap for high-protein pasta makes this a mac you can feel good about indulging in. Pair this with grilled blackened chicken (page 122) for some added heat and the perfect high-protein meal or with some Macro-Friendly Instant Pot Chili (page 67) for the best chili mac.

NUTRITION	MACROS PER SERVING	OTHER NUTRITION
Total Servings: 6	**Protein:** 23 g	**Cholesterol:** 50 mg, **Sodium:** 377 mg, **Potassium:** 473 mg, **Dietary Fiber:** 3 g, **Sugars:** 5 g
Serving Size: 190 grams	**Carbs:** 28 g	
Calories: 354	**Total Fat:** 19 g	

8 oz (226 g) uncooked chick-pea cavatappi pasta (Banza™)

½ cup (110 g) low-fat cottage cheese

1½ cups (355 g) whole milk

2 tbsp (28 g) salted butter

2 tbsp (16 g) all-purpose flour

Pinch of salt, plus more to taste

½ tsp garlic powder, plus more to taste

1 cup (85 g) shredded Cheddar cheese, at room temperature

1 cup (85 g) shredded reduced-fat sharp cheese, at room temperature

Ground nutmeg, to taste (optional)

Paprika, to taste (optional)

Cayenne pepper, to taste (optional)

Cook the pasta according to the package directions. While the pasta cooks, blend the cottage cheese in a high-speed blender, slowly adding ½ cup (120 g) of milk at a time until completely smooth.

When the pasta is cooked, drain it and set it aside.

Melt the butter in a large pan over medium heat. Add the flour and stir until combined into a paste. Stir and cook the paste for 1 minute. Slowly add the cottage cheese mixture while whisking. Whisk in the salt and garlic powder. Simmer and whisk for about 3 minutes until everything is well combined and the sauce begins to thicken.

Once the sauce has thickened, lower the heat to low. Slowly add the cheese as you mix until all the cheese has melted and a cheese sauce has formed. Add the pasta and mix everything together. To add extra spice to your mac and cheese, season it with nutmeg, paprika, cayenne pepper or extra garlic powder.

NOTE: Additional recipe alert! Make the cheese sauce by itself without the pasta, then add extra seasonings to taste like my blackened or cajun seasoning or add fresh salsa and mix together. Pair it with your favorite chips or veggies for a super cheesy dip.

Fancy Green Beans

Holidays are some of my favorite times to be in the kitchen. I love to make the classics that everyone expects, and this fancy green bean recipe is just that. With the perfect amount of buttery garlic crunch, this dish looks as appealing as it tastes. It will be stunning on your holiday table or any day of the week.

NUTRITION	MACROS PER SERVING	OTHER NUTRITION
Total Servings: 6 **Serving Size:** 100 grams **Calories:** 99	**Protein:** 3 g **Carbs:** 10 g **Total Fat:** 6 g	**Cholesterol:** 10 mg, **Sodium:** 8 mg, **Potassium:** 256 mg, **Dietary Fiber:** 3 g, **Sugars:** 4 g

1 lb (454 g) fresh green beans, ends trimmed

2 tbsp (28 g) unsalted butter

¼ cup (30 g) sliced almonds

3 cloves garlic, minced

1 shallot, thinly sliced and chopped

Fresh cracked pepper

Bring a large pot of salted water to a boil. Add the green beans and cook for 3 to 4 minutes until they are crisp-tender. Immediately transfer the green beans to a large bowl of ice water to halt the cooking process and to preserve their vibrant color. Drain the green beans and slightly dry them off with a paper towel. Set them aside.

In a large skillet, melt the butter over medium heat. Add the almonds and cook for 3 to 4 minutes, stirring frequently, until they are golden brown and fragrant. Use a slotted spoon to remove the almonds from the skillet. Set them aside on a plate.

To the same skillet, add the garlic and shallot. Sauté for 2 to 3 minutes until they are softened and fragrant. Add the green beans and toss to coat them with the garlic-shallot mixture. Cook for 2 to 3 minutes until the green beans are heated through.

Transfer the green beans to a serving platter or individual plates. Sprinkle the toasted almonds over the top, then season with pepper to taste.

NOTES: Add sliced brown mushrooms to the garlic and shallot, then combine with the greens beans to make this dish even fancier. Or top the green beans with freshly squeezed lemon juice for a bright summery flavor.

Sliced Cucumber Salad

This light, refreshing salad is perfect for warm weather. It features crisp, cool cucumbers sliced into thin rounds and paired with a simple, tangy dressing made with vinegar, coconut aminos and a touch of sweetness. It's a refreshing, healthy side dish that's easy to prepare, and it's perfect for any occasion from picnics to potlucks. Just remember to slice those cucumbers as thin as you possibly can!

NUTRITION	MACROS PER SERVING	OTHER NUTRITION
Total Servings: 6	**Protein:** 1 g	**Cholesterol:** 0 mg, **Sodium:** 382 mg, **Potassium:** 128 mg, **Dietary Fiber:** 1 g, **Sugars:** 7 g
Serving Size: 126 grams	**Carbs:** 12 g	
Calories: 61	**Total Fat:** 1 g	

¼ cup (60 g) coconut aminos

1 tbsp (15 g) rice vinegar

1 tbsp (15 g) lite pancake syrup or honey

½ tsp grated ginger

1 clove garlic, minced

1 tbsp (8 g) sesame seeds (plus more for serving, optional)

2 medium cucumbers, thinly sliced (150 g)

1 cup (75 g) shredded carrots

½ small red onion, thinly sliced (100 g)

Salt and pepper, to taste

In a small bowl, whisk together the coconut aminos, vinegar, syrup, ginger, garlic and sesame seeds. To a large bowl, add the cucumbers, carrots, onion, salt and pepper.

Pour the dressing over the cucumber mixture and toss until everything is well coated. Cover the bowl and place it in the fridge for at least 30 minutes to allow the flavors to meld together.

When ready to serve, give the salad a quick toss and garnish it with sesame seeds, if desired.

Cauliflower Quinoa Tabbouleh

The seasonings in tabbouleh harmonize so well together. The mint and the parsley with a drizzle of olive oil really creates something magical. I've shaken things up here by swapping out traditional bulgur wheat and using instead a combination of protein-rich quinoa and cauliflower rice. The result is a refreshing, satisfying salad perfect with lunch or as a side dish.

NUTRITION	MACROS PER SERVING	OTHER NUTRITION
Total Servings: 10	**Protein:** 3 g	**Cholesterol:** 0 mg, **Sodium:** 24 mg, **Potassium:** 294 mg,
Serving Size: 117 grams	**Carbs:** 23 g	**Dietary Fiber:** 3 g, **Sugars:** 3 g
Calories: 114	**Total Fat:** 6 g	

½ cup (87 g) uncooked quinoa

1 cup (240 g) water

½ tsp salt

1 small head cauliflower, cut into florets (450 g)

1 cup (60 g) finely chopped fresh parsley

1 cup (96 g) finely chopped fresh mint leaves

1 cup (150 g) cherry tomatoes, halved or quartered

½ small red onion, finely chopped (100 g)

½ English cucumber, diced (190 g)

¼ cup (60 g) olive oil

¼ cup (60 g) fresh lemon juice from 1 large lemon

1 clove garlic, minced

Salt and pepper, to taste

1 lemon, or more to taste

Red pepper flakes (optional)

Rinse the quinoa in a fine-mesh strainer under cold running water to remove any bitter outer coating. In a small saucepan, combine the quinoa, water and salt. Bring it to a boil, then reduce the heat to low and simmer, covered, for 12 to 15 minutes, or until the quinoa has absorbed the water and is tender. Remove the saucepan from the heat and let the quinoa stand, covered, for 5 minutes. Fluff the quinoa with a fork and set it aside to cool.

In a food processor or blender, pulse the cauliflower florets until they reach a rice-like consistency. Be careful not to overprocess the cauliflower.

In a large serving bowl, combine the quinoa, cauliflower rice, parsley, mint, tomatoes, onion and cucumber. Toss the ingredients gently to combine.

In a small bowl, whisk together the oil, lemon juice, garlic, salt and pepper to create the dressing. Pour the dressing over the tabbouleh and toss gently to coat the ingredients evenly. Season the tabbouleh with the salt and pepper to taste.

Refrigerate the tabbouleh for at least 30 minutes to allow the flavors to meld together. Before serving, top it with the juice of one lemon and mix well to combine. Serve with additional lemon and red pepper flakes for added heat, if desired.

Mom's "Best Ever" Peanut Noodles

Any time we had a summer barbecue or family gatherings growing up, my mom made a batch of her "best ever peanut noodles." I made some edits to make it higher in protein and lower in fat while remaining faithful to her amazing creamy, spicy, salty dish that keeps you wanting more. Bring this to your next gathering—just be sure to bring the recipe too, as you'll need it when everyone starts asking for it.

NUTRITION	MACROS PER SERVING	OTHER NUTRITION
Total Servings: 10	**Protein:** 9 g	**Cholesterol:** 0 mg, **Sodium:** 225 mg, **Potassium:** 256 mg, **Dietary Fiber:** 5 g, **Sugars:** 9 g
Serving Size: 170 grams	**Carbs:** 36 g	
Calories: 205	**Total Fat:** 3 g	

14½ oz (411 g) spaghetti (Barilla® Protein Plus)

½ cup (40 g) shredded carrots

½ cup (60 g) sliced celery

½ cup (50 g) sliced green onions (plus more for serving, optional)

1 small red bell pepper, thinly sliced

½ head cabbage, core removed and shredded (300 g)

1 oz (28 g) salted peanuts, chopped

Red pepper flakes, for serving (optional)

Peanut Sauce

2 tbsp (16 g) powdered peanut butter (PB Fit®)

½ cup (120 g) water

2 tsp (10 g) olive oil

3 cloves garlic, minced

1½ tsp red pepper flakes

½ cup (125 g) hoisin sauce

1–2 tbsp (15–30 g) lime juice

Cook the spaghetti according to the package directions. Drain and let it cool completely. This is important so that the heat doesn't make the sauce runny.

To make the peanut sauce, in a small mixing bowl, stir together the powdered peanut butter and water to create a peanut butter consistency. In a separate bowl, whisk the oil, garlic, red pepper flakes, hoisin and lime juice. Add the oil mixture to the peanut butter mixture. Stir to combine until smooth.

In a large bowl, combine the carrots, celery, green onions, bell pepper, cabbage and cooled spaghetti. Add one-third of the peanut sauce and start mixing to coat. Add another third of the sauce and continue mixing. You can add in the remaining sauce or save it for topping right before you serve.

Top the noodles with the peanuts and any extra toppings such as green onions or red pepper flakes. Serve at room temperature.

OH SNAP MACROS APP

Not sure how to incorporate these meals and more from the website into your daily macros? Let us help you with the Oh Snap Macros app! This app revolutionizes your meal-planning experience by tracking your macros effortlessly. It showcases a wide array of recipes, curated by Danielle, to cater to your specific nutritional needs. Seamlessly integrated macro tracking enables you to maintain a balanced diet without compromising on taste.

With the Oh Snap Macros app, you get mouthwatering recipes and you'll stay on track with your health goals. Embrace a hassle-free, macro-friendly menu, as the app does the heavy lifting of macro calculations for you!

Scan the QR code with your phone to download the app and start tracking!

ACKNOWLEDGMENTS

Writing a cookbook is exactly what they say it is . . . a labor of love! It took some incredible people to make this book come to life, and I am so thankful for every single one of you.

To my extraordinary Oh Snap Macros community, thank you for trusting me in your kitchen and being the kindest and biggest cheerleaders. Without your appetite for macro-friendly food, this cookbook would be as bland as unseasoned tofu.

To Mariam Baxter, my culinary comrade: Thank you for your willingness to test, taste and critique throughout the writing of this book. Your taste buds must be Olympic athletes by now!

To Kennedy Cagnina, the media manager extraordinaire: Thank you for your tireless editing and for testing even the most questionable concoctions. Our decades-long friendship means the absolute world to me.

To Bret Heiser, my incredible cheerleader, friend and shoulder to lean on: Your support has been as vital as the perfect seasoning to a dish. Your friendship is like a pinch of salt—it brings out the best in everything and I'd be lost without you.

To my husband, my biggest cheerleader, taste tester and best friend: Thank you for supporting me through this wild journey. You've been the sous-chef of my dreams and the secret ingredient to my success. I love you so much.

To my beautiful daughters, who inspire me every day: Thank you for making me realize that creating delicious and nutritious food is about nourishing those we love and creating memories that last a lifetime.

To the fabulous Page Street Publishing team, including the one and only Emily Archbold: Thank you for turning my kitchen scribbles into a beautiful, droolworthy book.

To my mom, dad and sister: Your endless support means the world to me. And to my mom, I can just imagine your pride as you tell the world that your daughter's cookbook is available in bookstores everywhere—that thought keeps me going. I miss you dearly; this one's for you, Mom.

Let's raise a macro-friendly toast to everyone who has been a part of this adventure. May your days be filled with perfectly portioned meals and laughter that's as infectious as the aroma of freshly baked lemon-blueberry oatmeal. Cheers!

ABOUT THE AUTHOR

Danielle Lima wears many hats: wife, mother, blogger, friend, sister, daughter. She is the creator and mastermind behind Oh Snap Macros, a food blog where she shares her recipes that revolve around macronutrients. Her goal through her blog is to create meals for people like her: people who are busy, who are working, who are parents, who want to be health-conscious without letting it consume their lives. It's for people who view food as something to be enjoyed and relished while understanding that food fuels our bodies and can make us the best version of ourselves. Her goal is to bring quick, easy but completely craveable dishes to your table. Danielle currently lives in Anchorage, Alaska, with her husband and two daughters.

INDEX